Frederick Grimke

The *Rights* of WOMEN in a *Democratic* REPUBLIC

A Modern Edition,
Introduced with Commentary by
DONALD F. MELHORN JR.

ARCHWAY
PUBLISHING

Archway Publishing books may be ordered through booksellers or by contacting:

Archway Publishing
1663 Liberty Drive
Bloomington, IN 47403
www.archwaypublishing.com
1 (888) 242-5904

Because of the dynamic nature of the Internet, any web addresses or links contained in this book may have changed since publication and may no longer be valid. The views expressed in this work are solely those of the author and do not necessarily reflect the views of the publisher, and the publisher hereby disclaims any responsibility for them.

Any people depicted in stock imagery provided by Thinkstock are models, and such images are being used for illustrative purposes only.
Certain stock imagery © Thinkstock.

ISBN: 978-1-4808-2928-2 (sc)
ISBN: 978-1-4808-2929-9 (hc)
ISBN: 978-1-4808-2930-5 (e)

Library of Congress Control Number: 2016906974

Print information available on the last page.

Archway Publishing rev. date: 8/12/2016

To Marshall and Melhorn, and its People

Contents

Illustrations

Foreword

Judith Richards Hope,
First woman Fellow of the Harvard Corporation

Donald F. ("Frank") Melhorn and I met in July, 1964, when I applied for a job with his Toledo, Ohio law firm, then named Marshall, Melhorn, Bloch & Belt. (The "Melhorn" at that time was Frank's father.) I had returned home after graduating from the Harvard Law School, one of fifteen women in a class with more than five hundred men. All of our professors had been men, including our tax professor and Dean, Erwin Griswold. At that time, there were just two ladies' rooms on the campus, neither of which was located in the main classroom building, Langdell Hall. Still, the fifteen of us made it through. We were eager to graduate and to find our place in the world of law.

I had, I thought, planned carefully: I had a good record from a great law school, top grades from high school and college, and a home town advantage: my mother, with a Masters degree in psychiatric social work, was the respected supervisor of the local court of domestic relations. What's more, the law was now clearly in my favor: after months of rancorous debate, Congress had passed the Civil Rights Act of 1964, outlawing discrimination based on race, color, religion, **sex,** or national origin.

The Marshall, Melhorn interview seemed to go well. The lawyers there were welcoming and polite. They were also curious – they had never met a woman lawyer, and had definitely never considered working with one. Frank, who graduated from

Harvard Law four years ahead of me, had just returned from active duty in the U.S. Navy to become the firm's lowest ranking associate. He was particularly supportive of my application. I have never forgotten his encouragement. The lawyers I met that day praised my academic record. Several of them seemed even more interested in the fact that I had ranked at the top of the Ohio state speed typing contest when I was fifteen years old, typing 120 correct words per minute on a manual typewriter. In the end – and notwithstanding the proscriptions of the recent Civil Rights Act, Marshall, Melhorn did not offer me a job: "Our clients would never agree to a woman" working on their matters.

I submitted my resume to other fine law firms in Toledo, Columbus, Cleveland, and Cincinnati. The results were exactly the same: "We have never hired a woman lawyer, and we don't intend to change that policy any time soon." The other fourteen women from my class were having similar difficulties. Yet, against the odds we faced in the 1960's, all of us eventually landed good jobs. Every one of us has had a remarkable career. I am in awe of the courage, persistence, and plain raw talent of the women in the Harvard Class of 1964. We jumped over obstacles, or, when that failed, just crawled around them. Even when friends and relatives thought we should quit, we never gave up. A dozen years ago, I recounted our personal histories in my book *"Pinstripes & Pearls,"* published by Scribner.

There are thirteen of us left. Now in our 70's, we continue to serve our communities, our country, and the law. Arlene Lezberg Bernstein hung out her shingle as a specialist in family law. She was a successful sole practitioner near Boston for over fifty years. Diana Gordon is a professor of law at the City College of New York.

Marjory Freincle Gibson is head of her own mediation firm in Oakland, California, having served as a City Council Member and the Vice Mayor of Oakland for many years. Alice Pasachoff Wegman recently retired as Counsel to the EPA's Environmental Appeals Board. She and her husband Dick are international champions at duplicate bridge. Barbara Margulies Rossotti, a highly regarded corporate lawyer, went on to chair both her prominent Washington, D.C. law firm, and the Board of her undergraduate *alma mater*, Mt. Holyoke. She continues to oversee the Charles O. and Barbara M. Rossotti Scholarship fund at Georgetown University. At the time of her death in 2014, Sonia Faust had just retired from her position as Hawaii's Assistant Attorney General for Land and Transportation. Judith W. Rogers has had an illustrious career in public service: Assistant United States Attorney, Attorney General of the District of Columbia, Chief Judge of the District of Columbia Court of Appeals, and, since 1994, Judge on the United States Court of Appeals for the D.C. Circuit, the second highest court in the land. Rosemary Cox Masters left the law and became a psychotherapist. After the tragic 2001 attack on Manhattan's World Trade Center, she founded the Trauma Studies Center at New York City's Institute for Contemporary Psychiatry, where she still serves as Director while also maintaining an active private practice. Patricia Scott Schroeder was the first woman from Colorado to be elected to Congress and also the first to serve on the House Armed Services Committee. When a new colleague there asked how she could be a legislator at the same time as being the mother of two small children, she gave an historic answer: "I have a brain and a uterus and I use them both." Pat ran for President of the United States in 1987. She retired from Congress after 24 years, having never lost an election. She next headed the American Book Publishers Association, and currently chairs the English Speaking Union. Ann Dudley Goldblatt, a bombshell debutant from Pasadena, left her promising career as a Wall Street corporate lawyer when she married her law school beau and moved to Chicago. After bearing three children, she returned to school and earned a Masters of Law in medical ethics. Until last year, Ann Dudley was a lecturer in the Social Sciences, Biological Sciences and Humanities Division of the University of Chicago while, at the same time, serving as associate director of the MacLean Center for Clinical Medical Ethics there.

I left the full time practice of law a decade ago, but remain a counselor for several clients. I continue to serve on corporate Boards, including the Union Pacific Corporation, where I was the first woman elected to the Board of Directors in the railroad's 150 year history. As it has turned out, I have been the first woman in a number of roles: the first woman partner in my law firm, Paul, Hastings, Janofsky & Walker, and the first to serve on its Executive Committee; the first on the Board of the Zurich Reinsurance Company, and the first woman in over three and a half centuries to be selected for the Harvard Corporation, "The President and Fellows of Harvard College", the University's senior governing board.

My female law school classmates and I have lived Grimke's audacious dream of more than a century ago: women can do the work if they are given a chance. We will gather again soon at Harvard Law School to dedicate the formerly grubby ladies' room in the basement of Austin Hall on the far south side of the campus to the Harvard Law women of the future.

Frank Melhorn's brilliant introduction to this much anticipated republication of Grimke's prescient but, until now, little known essay reminds us of our debt to the centuries of effort undertaken by thousands of visionary women and men to ensure equal opportunity for women. It is no longer odd to see a woman in the courtroom, in the board room, in the operating room, in the Cabinet, in the Congress. When I was growing up in Ohio, there was only one woman judge in the federal court system, Florence Ellinwood Allen. Named to the United States Court of Appeals for the 6th Circuit by President Franklin Delano Roosevelt in 1934, she was the first woman to serve on any federal court in the United States. Now, of course, there are three women Justices on the United States Supreme Court, in addition to retired Justice Sandra Day O'Connor. Thirty-five percent of the Federal appellate court judges are women, as are thirty-three percent of federal trial judges. Four of the seven justices of the Ohio Supreme Court are women, including its Chief Justice, Maureen O'Connor. At my alma mater, Dean Martha Minnow presides over a faculty one third of whom are women, as are half of Harvard's law students. There are now twenty seven ladies' rooms on the Harvard law campus, including six in the main classroom building, Langdell.

I am deeply grateful that Frank Melhorn's life-long interest in legal history and equal rights led him to discover Frederick Grimke's historic essay, ***"The Rights of Women in a Democratic Republic."*** Now it is republished in an informative modern edition which will add greatly to the literature on women's rights. It is a farsighted work that, had my classmates and I known of it when we started out, would have helped us crack open the door to what has proved to be one of the greatest extensions of freedom in our lifetime. My women classmates and I stand on the shoulders of those who, like Frederick, foresaw women's potential. Without them and scores like them, today's women would never have been able to break through.

Preface

My perception of the very modest position I occupy on the periphery of historical scholarship originated, as I now believe, with a remark the Navigator made after a nighttime encounter with an uncharted seamount, in South Pacific waters not much traveled by deep-draft vessels since World War II. A combination of very lucky happenstances had enabled the ship to be stopped in time – and it takes a long time to stop an aircraft carrier – with just thirty feet or so under the keel. Some of the officers on the bridge that night (as a newbie "under instruction" my job was to "stay the hell out of the way") gathered the next morning to re-examine the chart for any indication of the hazard we had so narrowly avoided. All we found were a few notations in places too far distant to have suggested any alteration of course, of shoals tentatively marked "P.D." (position doubtful), or "E.D." (existence doubtful). They were based on random encounters during the war, when many ships were in the area, but the mariners who sailed them were urgently preoccupied. And mostly they lacked the skill which only long practice provides, for making sextant observations precise enough to yield positions by celestial navigation, the only means of position-finding then available, that were sufficiently accurate to be used in chart-making. (An observational error of a tenth of a degree, for example, has a six nautical mile positional effect.) It might have been my own, even worse performance in familiarization training with the instrument, which prompted my recalling the Navigator's response when someone expressed surprise that the shoal we encountered had not been observed before. "What someone observed doesn't matter," he said. "It's what was <u>reported</u> that counts."

Reporting unexpected findings informatively enough to be counted for inclusion in a body of historical knowledge over which scholars preside, has since become an avocation in my life.* But such reporting does not entitle *me* to be counted in the company of those scholars, for the learning of professional historians is more broadly-based than mine, and their judgments in matters within their competence are incomparably more authoritative. That is particularly true for the academic field of women's studies, as to which I have no professional qualifications.

For the report made by the present endeavor I have had a lot of help. The University of Michigan's William L. Clements Library, repository of the Weld-Grimké Family Papers, could not have been more welcoming all during the years when my unevenly paced research took place. Of staff members now retired I recall with special gratitude the interest the Clements Library's then director John Dann took early-on in my work, when the key to understanding the connection between Sarah Grimké's feminist writings and her brother Frederick's political treatise had not yet been discovered;

---

* See, e.g. Donald F. Melhorn, Jr., *"Lest We Be Marshall'd": Judicial Powers and Politics in Ohio, 1806-1812* (University of Akron Press, 2003); Melhorn, "A Moot Court Exercise: Debating Judicial Review Prior to *Marbury v. Madison*," *Constitutional Commentary* 12 (Winter 1995): 327-354; Melhorn, "The First Trial in Ohio that Lasted More Than a Day," *Ohio Lawyer* 9 (Jul.-Aug. 1995) 16-17, 31; Melhorn, "Jupiter's Sons: Greene County's Citizen Judges and the Sweeping Resolution, 1810-1814," in Michael Les Benedict and John F. Winkler, eds., *The History of Ohio Law* (Ohio University Press, 2004), 1:238-66; and Melhorn, "Richardson, Ft. Meigs, and the Story of Metoss," *Northwest Ohio Quarterly* 69 (Summer 1997):133-60.

and the assistance Barbara DeWolfe, now Curator Emeritus of Manuscripts, provided by arranging for production of a complete set of photocopies of Sarah's notebooks, available to all readers, of which I made considerable use. I also formed valuable acquaintances with Brian Dunnigan, the Library's Assistant Director, along with Clayton Lewis, Curator of Graphics, who helped me find illustrations, and Janet Bloom, Research Services Specialist, who with great patience met my requests for copying pages of the notebooks with the care and clarity required for publication. Invariably courteous but firm as they enforced rules essential for its secure and efficient operation, the Clements Library's doorkeepers and reading room supervisors also contributed substantially to the pleasure of my working there.

Steps away from the Clements, the University of Michigan's Harlan Hatcher Graduate Library was my principal source for period newspapers and pamphlets preserved on digital or microform media, and for journals and books found only in major universities' main libraries, of which the Hatcher is one of the best. I am grateful for the access to its collections I had as a reader without any University of Michigan affiliation, and I am indebted to the Hatcher's reference librarians who assisted me. Among those who went far beyond the call of their duties were Judith Avery, now retired, who established a key research finding by her discovery in the University of Wisconsin library of a rare issue of a feminist journal, *The Lily*, published after the period covered by supposedly complete microform collections; and Scott Dennis, who stayed on after his shift at the main floor reference desk to help me supply a single missing page number for a work cited in an endnote.

I knew before I started on this project that research into Frederick Grimke's life as a Yale student (Class of 1810) would provide welcome opportunities to re-visit that university's Sterling Memorial Library, in which the Manuscript and Archives Division is the repository of works and memorabilia relating to the Yale's own history. Records of campus debates in which late eighteenth and early nineteenth-century undergraduates engaged are fascinating sources of evidence of an individual's contact with an issue, first encountered as a student, that he would confront again in historically significant later life. I had previously discovered such evidence for George Tod (Class of 1795), a subject of two of my previous reporting efforts. But I did not yet know of the substantial interest in women's issues taken by Yale's presidents when Tod and Frederick Grimke were undergraduates – Ezra Stiles from 1778 to 1795) and Timothy Dwight from 1795 to 1817, respectively. Research in pursuance of this Grimke project was aided by knowledgeable Manuscripts and Archives staff members, including Chief Research Archivist Judith Ann Schiff, and Bill Landis, head of Public Services.

The American Antiquarian Society library in Worcester, Massachusetts, was a rich source for illustrations. For copies of two which appear in this book I am indebted to its Image Rights and Design Librarian, Jacklyn Donovan Penny.

Ohio State University faculty members contributed, at different times, encouragement and valuable suggestions. A legal history seminar which met informally at the law school, then led by Professor of History Michael Les Benedict, provided a forum for exploring some of the questions raised by *Rights of Women* shortly after my discovery of the essay. Much later, after it had become the subject of a book draft, David Stebenne, Professor of History and Law and a collaborator in concurrent efforts to promote wider interest in Ohio's legal history, introduced me to his colleague Professor Joan E. Cashin, who supplied an important insight into the significance of Grimké family sibling relationships.

Richard S. Walinski, a Toledo attorney with impressive scholarly attainments, pointed out flaws in my work correctable by editing. Megan E. Cross, who subsequently performed that function with a high degree of technical competence, also contributed substantive advice concerning matters on which I had invited her to comment.

Support in the end game as the work was almost ready for publication was very generously provided by Judy Hope, in a Foreword which recounts our first meeting, and by my Yale classmate Sam Chauncey, whose long service in the University's administration contributed importantly to Yale's response to challenges recent decades have brought.

My dedication of this book to "Marshall and Melhorn and its People" is an inadequate expression of thanks for the support of my law firm (more than a hundred years old, its name-sake partners are deceased). It has provided not only a well-equipped workplace, but also the services and expertise of its people, many of whom have given generously of their time and effort. I am particularly indebted to three of my partners – Jennifer Dawson, for critically reviewing parts of my drafts; Stephen Evans, for guidance as to intellectual property matters; and Roman Arce, for translating a relevant Spanish text. Without the patient assistance of Devon Gordon, the firm's information services manager, the frustrations arising out of my technical shortcomings could not have been overcome. Barbara Avery, our firm's librarian, responded readily to requests for help in research. My secretary, Mary Miller, has been a productivity multiplier in this, as in other endeavors.

I must also acknowledge support of a kind any author is especially fortunate to have, from people who listen patiently when he talks about his work, not because they are the least bit interested in it, but because it's something they sense his need to share. I will not name those who have had to endure this from me only once or twice, which is commendable but not heroic. Among those who have had to submit to it more frequently are my partner Paul Kraus, whose office is next to mine; Ken Pardiac, an Ann Arbor friend who was usually good for meeting up for a beer after I had finished the day's research on the project and didn't really need to hear about it; and Ryan Schoen, a former neighbor and longtime friend.

Introduction:
A Work "Too Unpopular to Suit the Public"

"I had no idea I would find it so difficult to get it into circulation," Sarah Grimké wrote to a friend in the feminist movement, telling of her efforts to find a publisher for her brother Frederick Grimke's provocative essay, *The Rights of Women in a Democratic Republic.* Frederick (who spelled their family name without the accent on the last letter) lived in Chillicothe, Ohio. After his resignation from the Ohio Supreme Court in 1842, he had devoted his life to interests in political and social theory. Self-absorbed and eccentric, a lifelong bachelor, he was famously uncomfortable in female society. But he was immensely proud of his sisters, Sarah and Angelina, whose personal accomplishments in the service of abolitionist and feminist causes inspired his vision of the future of women in America. "This is a question of infinitely more importance than is generally supposed," his essay began. "The placing of men and women upon precisely the same footing in political society will be one of the greatest revolutions in human affairs since the beginning of society."[1]

One of the publication prospects Sarah approached rejected the essay "because it would make so small a book." But Sarah did not want it in a pamphlet, "because pamphlets are despised, and because it could not in that form have circulation beyond our own circle." So she submitted it to *Putnam's*, a magazine with a general circulation that later became *Atlantic Monthly.* That submission brought another rejection: the magazine's editors found the essay's message "too unpopular to suit the public."[2]

Illustration 1. Horace Greeley and Feminists, *Yankee Notions,* Oct. 1853

Sarah then called on an influential supporter, "one of the first to espouse our cause," who had given the women's rights movement sympathetic coverage in his *New York Tribune*. But Horace Greeley told her that "so much had already been printed" about the movement that "nothing new could be said." Recounting their meeting in the same letter to her friend, Sarah said she thought "poor Mr. Greeley" was "worn out with espousing Reforms." Whether he actually read *Rights of Women* is unknown. But Sarah did not give up easily. She was "discouraged," she told her friend Harriot Hunt, "but determined to persevere until I get it into some Periodical." Sarah's letter is dated "February 1st"; an internal reference and other correspondence reveals the year, 1857.[3]

Dr. Harriot Hunt had practiced medicine in Boston since 1835; she was one of the nation's first female physicians. Her autobiography, *Glances and Glimpses; or Fifty Years Social, Including Twenty Years Professional Life*, was soon to be published and would be dedicated to Sarah.[4] Hunt's publisher, the one who thought *Rights of Women* would make "too small a book," was one of the first prospects Sarah approached with the essay. In a subsequent letter to Hunt, written in June, 1857, she reported that "brother's Essay is still on hand. I cannot tell what is best about it as I cannot get it into any popular periodical."[5]

The dating of Sarah's attempts to secure publication as having commenced during the winter of 1856-57 suggests that Frederick wrote the essay earlier in 1856.[6] In an April 22, 1857 letter he mentioned having given it to her on an occasion when they were together: that is likely to have been in the summer or fall of 1856. He had been preoccupied with revisions to his book-length political treatise, *Considerations Upon the Nature and Tendency of Free*

Institutions, published that year in a second edition.[7] But efforts to get *The Rights of Women* into print would not succeed in his lifetime.

The obstacle was the essay's conclusion. Frederick went beyond asserting that women were inherently as intelligent as men and fully equal in their potential for intellectual development – a claim beginning to gain acceptance even beyond feminist circles. It was in forecasting the consequence of women's realization of this potential that the work was radical. "[A] revolution is set on foot," Frederick wrote, "which although destined to be the most gradual as well as the most searching of all revolutions, no arm will have power to arrest." He predicted that American women – even married women with children – would eventually enter into all of the occupations and professions in which men engaged. Realization of this prediction would be gradual. "If society does actually undergo this change, it will not be in a single precipitous leap," he cautioned. "It will be after a long preparation for this new state of being. The present generation will only witness the discussion of it; the next will stop to ponder upon it; the third will probably enter upon the experiment of it."[8]

Foremost of the causes of this revolution which Frederick believed "will entirely alter the civil condition of women," was the "radical change" he saw beginning to take place in their access to higher education, a change that foretold "an entire alteration in [women's] disposition and character." "Painting, music, embroidery, no longer constitute the sum of their accomplishments. An academical course is now sought after, in which philosophy, science and history are taught." Although, as he thought, that development might come "at the expense of what in fashionable language are termed their personal charms," it would produce "strong minded young women, who like strong minded young men, know no other fashion than what is taught in the school of virtue and wisdom." But that achievement would not suffice. "Knowledge is inert, and genius dumb, when there is no outlet for it, no mode of exercising the mind practically, and to some end." Women's education may be "ever so thorough," Frederick wrote, "but it will be comparatively unprofitable unless the strong will, the will to do, is combined with the resources of knowledge, and this strong will never exists unless both the active and [the] intellectual powers are developed."[9]

Feminist leaders were making the same point. "Women, like men, must be educated with a view to action," wrote English novelist and economist Harriet Martineau, noting her disagreement with a clergyman reputedly sympathetic to women's causes, who "would have had any woman study anything that her faculties led her to, whether physical science, or law, government and political economy; but he would have her stop at the study."[10] "I shall be glad," said American activist Lucy Stone, "when liberty will be given to women to learn not from books alone but from the freedom to go out into the world's highway, and by actual conflict with life, learn the lessons that do not come from books."[11]

But mid-nineteenth century feminists' demands for equal vocational opportunities in occupations and professions for which higher education was requisite, hardly ever mentioned married women. The omission suggests a widespread assumption that their lives, especially when they included child raising, were incompatible with careers in those occupations. A committee report at a women's rights convention held at Worcester, Massachusetts in 1851 gave this assumption a positive spin, arguing that opening up "the practice of the professions" to women would provide an alternative for those women who were "unfitted and unqualified" for motherhood, tending to keep them "from assuming that sacred relation, prompted by unworthy motives."[12]

"Can they pursue the same avocations as men?" Frederick asked in *The Rights of Women* as he took up objections he anticipated from readers. For married women, he opined, the answer might depend on the number of children. If there were only one or two "the effect might simply [be] to produce a temporary suspension" of a woman's career in the workplace. Married women with a "numerous family would find their duties at home incompatible with a life abroad," but – and here he added a remarkably prescient qualification:

> At least this would be the case, until the system [in respect to women's participation in business and the professions] had become thoroughly established, and time and experience suggested many ways of overcoming difficulties which had not before been thought of. This is a very common occurrence. Individuals are unexpectedly thrown into a new situation, and this very circumstance inspires them with the intelligence and address which are necessary to accommodate themselves to it.[13]

Frederick next answered objections that mixed-sex workplaces would be dens of promiscuity, and that marital harmony would be disturbed by wives' careers outside the home. He ended his essay by challenging readers to follow his "vigorous analysis . . . to the truth, on whichever side it lies."[14]

Well, *Putnam's* editors were right. The essay's prediction of vocational equality for women would have been derided by a readership accustomed, in the 1850s, to seeing feminists' aspirations lampooned in grotesque portrayals of women in "men's" occupations.[15] An unsigned article *Putnam's* itself ran in March, 1853, shortly after the magazine commenced publication, challenged feminist demands as "ludicrously unworthy." "We are told by the soberest of our judges," the author intoned, "that if woman be admitted to forensic practice, it will soon be next to impossible to get a righteous decision from the bench, so inevitable a bias must her advocacy of any cause produce upon the judicial mind." Dreadful consequences were predicted for medicine and the ministry, should women enter either of those professions. Moreover, the article continued, "democracy has so shattered the dignity" of all professions, by making them "open to every vagabond who fancies that they may afford him a comfortable pasturage," that a professional life thus debased would be even more unfit for a woman - who was "not merely the mother of our children," but "the fountain of joy, of sweet contentment, of all that is refined in thought, of all that in generous and disinterested in affection, of all that is graceful and spontaneous and irresistible in manners."[16]

But a greater impediment to publication during Frederick's lifetime were the doubts he himself came to have about what he had written. In March, 1858 he confided to Sarah that he had "probably erred in supposing that the professions and the employments of civil life were within the appropriate domain of women," while assuring her that "there is really a vast field of exertion open to them which has never been explored, and which unless filled by them would never be filled at all." The same concern is reflected in subsequent letters to Sarah written during the ensuing twenty-one months. In July, 1859 he appealed to her directly, "to assist in enabling me to get rid of [my] doubts.[17]

Regrettably, however, only Frederick's side of this correspondence survives. His letters to Sarah are among the Weld-Grimké Family Papers, an archive with many items of the sisters' correspondence now an important holding of the William L. Clements Library at the University of Michigan. But we have none of Sarah's responding letters. One might expect her to have been reassuring, urging her brother to overcome his misgivings about a vision she would have been delighted to share. But nothing in Frederick's letters to her supports this expectation. On December 14, 1859, in the last letter in which he mentioned *The Rights of Women,* he told her that "the view which you take" of his work "must certainly be the correct one, that the destination of men and women is different."

For all the deficiencies of its transmission – for it comes to us only in Frederick's cryptic words of summation – Sarah's belief that the "destination" of men and women is fundamentally different in respect to potential for careers in higher-level occupations is intriguing. That it does not fit with the present widely held understanding of the cause for which Sarah's life is remembered makes the loss of her side of their correspondence especially grievous. It appears, moreover, that the loss is irretrievable. Had Frederick kept Sarah's letters he would not have had many places to put them in the premises he occupied in Chillicothe, in hotels where he boarded. They might have been in the "trunk full of old letters . . . mostly on professional business, and old law briefs & other legal papers," which Frederick's executor Allen G. Thurman found among his personal effects after his death. Thurman offered to have the trunk with its contents shipped to the sisters, who lived in New Jersey. But they apparently declined the offer, for no charge for any such shipment is listed among expenses of estate administration in the accounting filed in the probate court. If letters in which Sarah had expressed her views concerning Frederick's remarkable conclusion in his *Rights of Women* essay had been in the trunk, they were presumably discarded along with other contents that Thurman as executor saw no reason to retain.[18]

With Frederick's loss of confidence in what he had written came regressive changes in his aspirations for having *Rights of Women* published. At first he tried to convince himself that even if the essay's predictions were taken as preposterous, they might still be useful for shock effect. "Unless we claim the whole loaf," he told Sarah, "we shall not get half of a one."[19] Subsequently he requested that the essay be published anonymously.[20] He next made arrangements for posthumous publication. In his will, executed on September 1, 1862, he left two thousand dollars to finance a two-volume publication of all his works: the first volume to be a third edition of his political treatise *The Nature and Tendency of Free Institutions,* the second to contain miscellaneous writings, some not previously published. As one of those writings *Rights of Women* was specifically mentioned in the will, Frederick noting his "desire to alter [it] materially," but adding that "as it stands, it may excite dissension, and suggest new views, which constitute one half the merit of the composition."[21] But he would disown even that half. His last instruction, found in a note left with the essay's manuscript, was that it not be published at all. That instruction made it subject to a general direction in the will that writings not designated for publication be destroyed.[22]

Frederick died in Chillicothe on March 8, 1863. But it was not until 1871 when Thurman carried out his charge to publish a posthumous edition of Frederick's works. The edition was cheaply fabricated. It had no commercial sale. Copies Frederick had directed to be donated to institutional libraries might have been the edition's only distribution. In deliberate disregard of Frederick's direction in the note left with the essay's manuscript, Thurman included *The Rights of Women in a Democratic Republic* as the last work in the edition's second volume. But having been bound together with the first volume within the same set of book covers and without any table of contents, the second volume and its offerings were unlikely to be noticed. And so far as is known the essay was not so noticed – until recently. Its publication at the end of the second volume of Frederick's works is the only means by which it survived. All manuscript copies – the one Frederick left among his papers with the note attached, the one he gave to Sarah, and others she employed in her quest to have the work published in his lifetime – have been lost.

Allen Thurman never met either of the Grimké sisters. As Frederick's executor he communicated with them in letters addressed to Angelina, the residuary beneficiary of Frederick's estate. Four of those letters, and they are possibly all he wrote, are now among the Weld-Grimké Family Papers in the University of Michigan's Clements Library. Here again that archive contains only one side of what must have been an exchange of correspondence; missing are the sisters' letters responding to Thurman as he reported Frederick's death and subsequently the progress of settling the estate and causes of delay in getting the posthumous edition of Frederick's works published. None of Thurman's letters mentions the *Rights of Women* essay. Nor, so far as is known, is it mentioned in any letter either sister wrote to anyone else after Frederick's death. Indeed, there is no indication from any source that they, or Sarah in particular, ever took any further interest in it. Sarah died in 1873.

I found *Rights of Women* when I was asked to contribute entries on Frederick and another 19th century Ohioan, to the *Yale Biographical Dictionary of American Law.*[23] At first I thought of submitting the essay to a women's studies journal to publish as a curiosity, which, like Leonardo's notional flying machine, had no influence on subsequent realization of what it envisioned. But I could not have done even that little, without responding to two questions that even the briefest introduction of the work must address: what Sarah said about it when Frederick, coming to doubt what he had written, turned to her for reassurance; and how Thurman, his executor, came to include the essay in the posthumous edition of Frederick's writings despite his last wish that it not be published.

The late Veronica Wedgwood, a historian of the English revolution whose works are models of narrative exposition, once said that "an experiment in reconstructing" some curious happening or circumstance "as fully as possible . . . without attempting to prove any general point or demonstrate any theory whatsoever is a useful exercise," from which, sometimes, "unexpected clues are found to far more important matters."[24] What a pioneer of the American feminist movement of Sarah Grimké's stature thought about the striking conclusions of *The Rights of Women in a Democratic*

Republic is important, and an attempt to learn her views would surely be worth the effort. And, although a prospect of comparable benefit from attempting to explain Thurman's unauthorized action to publish the essay was not as evident, I couldn't very well pursue Sarah's part in the puzzle and not Thurman's. I didn't know who Allen G. Thurman was. I had never heard of him.

Anyone curious to learn the results of these investigations should first have read *Rights of Women*. To facilitate that I have placed it here, next following, along with the note Frederick left with the manuscript directing that it be suppressed.

I have followed this text with a broadly-based commentary which, in coming to recount Frederick's writing the essay and Sarah's involvement with it as literary agent and critic, leads to discoveries of substantial importance to the history of the American women's rights movement – all as Dame Veronica suggested.

The story of how Thurman came to spare *Rights of Women* from Frederick's order of suppression is left to be addressed at the end of this work, where the reader will become acquainted with Thurman himself, and find – perhaps unexpectedly – much of enduring significance about his life and times.

Illustration 2. Women's Rights, unsigned print, c. early 1850's.
Courtesy, American Antiquarian Society

The Rights of Women in a Democratic Republic

Originally published in *The Works of Frederick Grimke*
(Columbus, Ohio: Columbus Printing Co., 1871), 2:239-56

Note in Frederick Grimke's handwriting, appended to the manuscript and found after his death:

This essay is not to be published, as the views are pushed to an extreme. It is an effort to find out the truth, a preliminary investigation only. When re-written, and the views in some parts considerably modified, it will be published.

This is a question of infinitely more importance than is generally supposed. The placing of men and women upon precisely the same footing in political society will be one of the greatest revolutions in human affairs since the beginning of society. No question, therefore, which has ever been agitated, demands more thought, and a more unclouded judgment.

The capacity of the two sexes has been supposed to be different. I have given a great deal of consideration to this question, and am satisfied that the idea is without foundation. It is difficult, no doubt, where the training and education of the two has been different, to penetrate through the artificial exterior which has been superinduced, and to find out what the original capacities of the two are. But there are notwithstanding a sufficient number of facts to guide us. For first, boys and girls up to the time when their education ceases to be the same, afford no signs of an original difference of capacity. Second, where their education does not cease to be the same, but both are educated alike, as is now frequently the case, the faculties of one are developed in as high a degree as those of the other, especially if we make allowance for the sense of inferiority which the social position of females thrusts upon them, whatever their education may be. The confidence which men feel in themselves, knowing that all the avenues of intellectual distinction are open to them, and the want of confidence which women feel in consequence of their being closed to them, will necessarily produce a difference of mind and character, whatever their original capacities may be. Third, a great number of women have been distinguished for intellectual endowments, and for vigor and address in the active walks of life. The favorable position in which they have been placed, whether arising from fortuitous circumstances, from the happy turn which their education received, or from some peculiarity in their social condition, or from all three together, have been sufficient to develop faculties of a very high order.

But this by no means exhausts the question. The moral and intellectual faculties of the sexes may be equal, and yet they may be destined to different spheres. The first remarkable circumstance which strikes us, is that society everywhere and in all ages, exhibits the two as moving in very different spheres. A disposition of human affairs so general, almost invariable, that the departures from it are only exceptions to the rule, is above all other circumstances calculated to make us pause, and take a wide survey, before we decide a question which affects society so deeply. The present condition of women cannot be attributed to the fact that men have usurped the supremacy, that the control which they possess has been acquired wrongfully and fortuitously, not rightfully and legitimately. For how came the power to be originally usurped? By the supposition both in the beginning possessed equal capacities of all kinds? And yet there is no period when the distinction between the two sexes is more marked, than in the commencement of society. Among a tribe of hunters, a tribe of shepherds and in the patriarchal form of government, the vocations and pursuits of men and women are as distinct as in the refined and intellectual circles of Great Britain and the United States. There seems therefore at first, no way of accounting for the great differences in the condition of the two, but by supposing that there is some inherent law of our being, which has destined them to very different spheres.

It would not be extraordinary if such were the case. Human beings are enclosed on all sides by circumstances which act constantly and powerfully upon them, and prevent their leaping beyond a given condition. We see this exemplified in individuals of the same sex, no two of whom are alike, because each is controlled by some law which is proper to itself, and which mollifies the action of those causes which are common to the species. Even causes which are purely physical sometimes control the character and shape the whole destiny of life. If therefore men and women do possess equal capacities, and are yet destined to play very different parts, this would not at all be inconsistent with the general plan of providence. On the contrary, it would be in analogy with that plan, which everywhere shows variety and dissimilitude, amidst the greatest uniformity.

It is unnecessary, however, to indulge in mere speculation or conjecture. The question is perhaps capable of something like a precise determination. The causes which act upon individuals, and differ each from all others, are so minute, and so infinitely varied, as in many instances to be absolutely inscrutable. But this difficulty is not so great where the inquiry is confined to those laws which govern the character of classes. These are much fewer and more simple, and therefore more readily within the grasp of our understanding. They operate at one and the same time upon thousands, or millions who comprise that class, and therefore stand out prominently to observation.

The first two circumstances arising from the difference of sex, which are calculated to arrest attention, are child-bearing and nursing. These are the sole causes which have given to the life, and conduct of women, a direction totally different from that of men. For although there are many other causes of difference which may be detected, yet they are all subordinate to these two, all may be traced to them as their source.

The immediate effect of these is obvious. Confinement to the house and a constant devotion to their offspring during the period of infancy are the consequences. Men do not bear children and on that very account are less fitted to nurse them. And although in the mere intervals of nursing, fathers might take care of their children, they could not do so with as much skill and assiduity as mothers. There is an adaptedness to this duty on the part of mothers, which would be imperfectly imitated by fathers, independently of which, if both father and mother devoted themselves to the care of their infant children, a great deal of time would be lost to those who depend for subsistence on some out of door employment. It seems most fit, therefore, that care should be confided to one, and every circumstance seems to point to the mother as the one most eminently fitted for it. And as the personal care of the mother is indispensable during infancy, it is very naturally extended over the whole period of childhood. The care of the infant is a preparatory school for the more difficult and complicated cares which arise when the infant has emerged into childhood. These views acquire additional strength when it is recollected that the number of children may be from half a dozen to a dozen. A very considerable portion of life is then consumed in the nursing of infants, and in the cares which afterwards grow spontaneously out of this relation. Under such circumstances it would seem to be almost impossible for women to follow the same pursuits as men. We must not be startled because causes purely physical have produced this organization of domestic society. Causes of the same nature are perpetually at work to maintain the health of both body and mind, and to enable the whole of mankind to discharge the various duties of life. We can no more free ourselves from the laws which our physical being has imposed upon us, than the plant, or the animal can be made free of the laws which reign over them. But it is a happy circumstance, when these very laws become, as in the case of rational beings, the parent of the first disposition, and the most exalted virtues.

The causes to which I have referred, by confining women to the domestic hearth, produce a delicacy of frame, and character, which do not belong to men. And then commences the operation of moral causes, which constantly augment the distinction between the two. For first, this greater delicacy, and beauty, and the modesty which is naturally attendant upon them, causes females to be caressed, instead of the caressers. The masculine traits are then complete in the one sex, the feminine in the other. Man becomes an active, woman a passive being. All those occupations which require strength and activity of body or mind are assigned to the one, and those which are consistent only with great firmness of organization and character, to the other. Second, the inexpiable disgrace which attaches to women on any breach of chastity, contributes still further to heighten the distinction. An indiscriminate association with men would present instances of temptation so numerous, as would be difficult to resist. If yielded to, society would be converted into a pandemonium. They therefore voluntarily withdraw from public notice, and from all occupations which are common to men.

The marked attention and deference which are paid to females is a principal cause of the inferiority of mind, which manifests itself after they have attained to womanhood. This inferiority is acquired, not original. If the thing were reversed, and the same deference were paid to men, they would instantly sink in the scale as intellectual beings. Their character would assume the effeminate traits which belong to women. One reason undoubtedly why the sons of eminent men seldom fulfil the expectations which are formed of them, is that they enjoy from early youth some of the very deference which is paid to women as a class. Their fathers were perhaps turned out upon the world poor, and friendless, they were compelled to battle with all sorts of obstacles in order to win a reputation. Their sons have a name from the cradle. In youth they are noticed above all other young men, and this empty and imaginary distinction so beguiles their imagination and enfeebles their understandings, that instead of adding luster to their families they very often bring disgrace upon them. There are exceptions to this remark. Some youths of unusually fine mold, or whose condition has been counteracted by one cause or another, are goaded to an exertion, and redeem themselves from the imputation which is attached to the class. But these instances are as rare as of young ladies becoming distinguished as intellectual women. It is then the comparatively rugged life which men generally lead, the self- reliance and self-command to which they are inured, the having no name or reputation which they do not win for themselves, which cultivates in them more strength both of mind and body. And it is to causes entirely the reverse that we must attribute the delicacy and feebleness of women. Instead of being subjected to the toil of body and mind, to which men are exposed, they are indulged with the tranquil retreat of home: their path instead of being beset with difficulties is strewed with roses; they are everywhere met with obsequiousness and deference, the emptiness they are unable, or unwilling to comprehend, until it is too late. In is not in the power of human nature to resist an influence which is so fascinating, however fatal it may be to the growth of vigorous qualities. "Love (says Madame De Stael, who was a most illustrious exception to these remarks) which is but an episode in the life of man, makes up the whole life of woman." Men who are accustomed to ruminate upon one idea, or one set of ideas, have their minds more or less shrunk, and compacted. And where one sentiment reigns supreme over the life of woman, the effect is similar, only more decisive in its operation.

This presents the greatest difficulty in the way of lifting women to higher civil condition. Will they consent to give up their present position in order to participate in the strife, and turmoil of society? It all depends upon themselves; an enlightened resolution taken by any considerable body of persons will always be victorious. There can be no doubt, that at no former period would women have consented to make the exchange, nor would they generally at the present day. But their education is now of a much higher order than was ever before known, and this may produce an entire alteration in their disposition and character. There are decided symptoms of this in the very remarkable conventions which are now frequently held in the United States. The landed proprietors of Europe exchanged the personal services of their retainers for a fixed rent. They lost the deference and respect which was before paid to them, but they augmented their wealth, and all the enjoyments to which wealth is tributary, at the same time that they rose immeasurably in the scale of intellectual beings. In order to manage their inferiors, who were no longer their vassals, education, ability, information were called into requisition, and no one who had lived in the times of the Tudors of England, or the Henrys of France, would recognize the present race of country gentlemen as the same with the past.

And this at once opens up views which are entirely new, and of a deeply interesting character. Causes are actually at work at the present day, which in all human probability will entirely alter the condition of women. No one who has been accustomed to ponder upon those events which are passing before his eyes, in preference to groping in the dark annals of antiquity, can fail to be struck with the thorough and radical chance which is taking place in the education of women. Lord Chesterfield in one of his letters remarks, that he had never known a woman who was able for a quarter of an hour to hold a conversation which contained a consecutive train of ideas. This was said about one hundred years ago. Superficial observations, flippant remarks, made up the whole matter of conversation. The reason is obvious: the being to whom deference is paid, before a title to it is acquired, is deprived of all self-reliance, and never passes through that stern discipline which is necessary to rouse and strengthen the intellectual faculties.

The remark of Lord Chesterfield is by no means inapplicable to female society of the present day, but in his time it was true without any qualification: at the present the exceptions to it are numerous and remarkable. During the last twenty years the minds of young women have been subjected to a training which formerly was unknown. Many parents now desire to give their daughters a more elevated education. Painting, music, embroidery, no longer constitute the sum of their accomplishments. An academical course is now sought after, in which philosophy, science, and history are taught. This revolution is by no means general. Those who live in fashionable life adhere to the old system: but among the great body of the middle class there is a decided tendency to the adoption of a more rational plan. And it is to this class that we may trace all the great revolutions which characterize the history of modern society. In Great Britain, and still more in the United States, the singular spectacle is now for the first time presented, of the middle class not only ruling the minds but molding the manners and influencing the fashion.

It may seem extraordinary that fathers should be willing to give their daughters an education so much more elevated than formerly, where the direct consequence would be sooner or later to undermine the supremacy of their own sex. But no one is able to see clearly to the end of a revolution. All suppose that they are foresighted enough to do so, but dim views, vague conjectures, are all they ever attain to. These never enable them to realize what is coming; and it is this realization, their personification of what we learn, which constitutes knowledge. This constitution of our nature bespeaks no defect: without it society would never move forward.

This revolution in the life of woman which has just been commenced, is precisely similar to one which has been before our eyes for more than half a century. Some of the most absolute of the European princes have been vying with each other in efforts to impart the elements of even a high education among their people. The consequences would seem to be obvious. Thrones and principalities must be shaken: but no reasoning would be of power sufficient to turn aside the efforts of these princes. They can no more free themselves from the delusion which is thrust upon them, than we can avoid seeing the moon larger in the horizon, than in the zenith, or than we can avoid seeing the earth and the firmament touch each other. After a revolution that has advanced to a certain point, reasoning is very easy to be comprehended, but it is too late. The institutions which have then risen up possess a self-motive power, which bids defiance to any interference from without. Precisely what the head of the state is now doing in the European commonwealths with regard to the people, the heads of families are also doing with regard to their daughters. As the first have aided unconsciously, and contrary to what they conceive to be their true interests, in elevating the condition of their subjects, the last are in like manner embarked in a scheme for strengthening the power of women. This last revolution, as I have already remarked, is more observable in the United States than anywhere else. The reason is obvious: the republican institutions of the country give women more influence over their husbands, and place children more upon a footing with their parents, so that the wishes of both mothers and daughters are listened to with more attention than formerly. Mothers frequently desire to give their daughters a higher education; but this is by no means so common as for the daughters to desire the same thing. These often at an early period of life feel an ambition of acquiring knowledge. They are perhaps entirely insensible of the consequences; that the acquisition may be at the expense of what in fashionable language are termed their personal charms. Or they may be strong minded young women, who like strong minded young men, know no other fashion than what is taught in the school of virtue and wisdom. But whether young women are sensible or not of all the consequences to which the acquisition of knowledge may lead, a great and permanent benefit is conferred upon society. The first class perhaps never improve upon what they have learned; the second continue to improve after they have entered upon the theatre of life. The last devote themselves actively to improve and extend the system, while the first simply oppose no resistance to the same course of education for their daughters. And with the aid of this combined influence a revolution is set on foot, which although destined to be the most gradual, as well as the most searching of all revolutions, no arm will have the power to resist.

But no system of education however complete, will be sufficient to capacitate the mind for the exercise of its original and independent powers, unless the active faculties are brought into play, and a sort of intellectual experience, if I may use the expression, is engendered. Knowledge is inert, and genius dumb, when there is no outlet for it, no mode of exercising the minds practically, and to some end. By this I by no means intend that all the educated minds must be turned out into active life, in order to put the last finish upon them. Far from it, the most prolific geniuses, the minds which have been devoted to speculation, have had a character eminently practical, and have stirred the minds of other men more deeply, and extensively than any other class. What they have done in the closet has always had reference to the world without. They have been men, and that very circumstance has brought them into frequent collision with other minds during the greater part of life. By this means they have been able to make an infinitude of observations which have a direct bearing upon the whole course of their speculations. They are enabled to measure their own capacities, and the capacities of others, and through the minds and actions of others to study out all the problems to the solution of which their attention is directed independently: of which the outward discipline to which they are thus subjected keeps their minds in a state of intense activity. These advantages are all denied to females. "Their education may be ever so thorough, but it will be comparatively unprofitable unless some field of active thought is laid open to them. Education, even in the case of men, amounts to little or nothing unless the strong Will, the will to do, is combined with the resources of knowledge, and this strong will never exists unless both the active, and intellectual powers are developed.

These remarks, so far, have been confined to the highest exercise of the understanding, speculative philosophy, because their application to that department of human exertion is less open to ordinary apprehension. Assuredly Locke, and Adam Smith, and Kant, although living within the walls of a college during the greater part of their lives, felt the influence of that discipline which grows out of the action of mind upon mind, as much as the lawyer, the physician, or the merchant. They possessed this advantage, if for no other reason, simply because they were men, and as such, felt that they had a right to enjoy it.

But with regard to every other species of knowledge, the rudiments of which are intended to be taught in schools, academies, and colleges, the truth of the foregoing remarks is obvious. The lawyer, the physician, the merchant, never know anything until they are enabled to verify their knowledge by actual experience. Knowledge is not ours; it is only on paper, unless we can realize it in some way or other.

Young ladies may be taught history, the laws of their country, mental philosophy, physiology, but it will all terminate in nothing unless some object is set before them upon which their knowledge may center. A happy concurrence of circumstances will form exceptions to this rule. Very distinguished women have risen up in modern times. But it was only because they were able partially to emerge from the condition in which they were born, and to enjoy some of the advantages of men. The residence of Madame De Stael was the resort of all the intellectual men of Paris during the closing scenes of the revolution, and nothing contributed more to impart a healthy tone to society, and to eradicate the moral dyspepsia which had affected all ranks, than the happy turn which was thus given to the tastes and pursuits of both the old, and the young.

It has been said that the reason why mathematical truths have a character of such absolute certainty is because the proofs are illustrated by figures which are capable of being described, or constructed in space. A triangle is drawn upon a board, precisely as it is conceived in the mind. But moral ideas are incapable of this exact representation. There is however to a great extent an imitation of this very process, in every other department of knowledge: and hence the distinction between what is purely speculative and what is reducible to practice. In law and medicine, in politics, in the mechanic arts, every principle is the subject of experiment, and although the experiment does not as in mathematics contain the principle without any mixture of what is foreign to it, it is notwithstanding of wonderful use in elucidating and fortifying out knowledge. This is precisely the advantage which men possess over women. The greater part of them are destined to the active walks of life, and in these they have an opportunity of constantly seeing their knowledge subjected to the test of experience. The knowledge of women, for want of this grand instrument of improvement, perishes as soon as it has blossomed; it never goes to seed as it were, and reproduces itself by embodiment. It is now necessary to return to the view which was first unfolded, in which the difficulties in the way of placing men and women socially and civilly on the same footing were referred to. These difficulties were designedly set forth, because the analysis of no question on which contradictory opinions are held, is ever complete unless there is an examination of both. An opinion however erroneous, which has taken deep root, must at least have a reason for its existence. The inquiry, how such an opinion came to prevail is therefore the true way of combating it, and of vindicating the contrary. I have remarked that the distinction originally between men and women was a consequence of the physical structure of the last; that women, not men, have children, and that nature had provided the former alone with the means of nourishing their offspring in infancy: that from these causes purely physical, sprung a great number of moral causes which contributed to confirm the distinction, and to create for the one a domestic life, for the other a public life. There may be the wisest reasons for the existence of a custom or institution at one period of society, and yet these reasons may cease to be wise at a different period. The rise of commonality in modern Europe is a striking example. It may have been an act of suicide on the part of the community to have entrusted the masses in the reigns of the Edwards and Henrys with the power they now possess in England: yet nothing is more certain than that the very possession of his power at the present day is the chief cause of the security and stability of the government.

The impediments in the way of introducing women into civil life do not arise from any inferiority of capacity. The average of intellect among them is undoubtedly equal to what it is among men. And as the standard of female education is becoming higher and higher, the way at least if open for lifting them above the condition in which they have hitherto been placed. If society does actually undergo this change it will not be a single precipitous leap. It will be after a long preparation for this new state of being. The present generation will only witness the discussion of it; the next will stop to ponder upon it; the third will perhaps enter upon the experiment of it. For there is always much to ponder upon before any innovation is made in the institutions of society, and it must be admitted that no occasion has ever occurred on which calm and enlightened reflection will be more necessary than on this. Most salutary changes in civil affairs are sometimes retarded, sometimes never succeed, because they are not accompanied with the due amount of reflection and the necessary preparation. It is this which constitutes their sole title to respect, and the indispensable condition of their adoption. They may then, and then only be introduced without placing the society in a state of revolution, and incurring danger for which no advantages can compensate. Fortunately this is an age of reflection, and it is precisely because it is so, that this great question is now undergoing discussion.

I will now take a rapid and succinct survey of the difficulties which oppose themselves to the elevation of women, in order to ascertain, or in order that the reader together with myself may ascertain whether these difficulties are insuperable. For this is the legitimate purpose of all discussion, to make the enlightened reader a party to our speculations, and if they be well founded, to redouble their force.

First, can any but mothers take care of their offspring, not merely in infancy but during the whole period of childhood: and if this duty naturally and necessarily devolves upon them, can they pursue the same avocations as men? Secondly, will the mixture of the sexes, the free and unrestrained association which will take place between them, lead to universal licentiousness? A change of dress may be one of the consequences of masculine character imparted to women, and this like many other apparently small things may be sufficient to revolutionize the manners. Third, will the social equality of man and wife produce jealousies, dissensions, calculated to destroy domestic happiness? Is it consistent with what we know of human nature that there should be two masters in one household? There are many other topics which will suggest themselves, but they are all subordinate to, and spring from those which I have mentioned. If we can surmount these, the difficulty is at an end.

First, the average proportion of births to marriages in the United States is about four and a half to one. In Europe it is of course less, and it will necessarily become less in the United States as society advances and the population becomes dense. If four and a half to one is the average proportion, many mothers will have a more numerous family than this proportion indicates, while others

will have a less, and some none at all. As for the last, the mere
distinction of sex presents no obstacle to their admission to the
rights of men, nor to their pursuing the same civil occupations,
if agreeable to them. Nor will it, where the births are only one
or two, nor even where the births are numerous, but the deaths
during infancy render the family small. In all these instances,
except where there are no children, the effect might be simply to
produce a temporary suspension of some of the new avocations
to which women were addicted; and in the other, not even to have
that effect. Only remove out of the way the great obstacle which
custom and public opinion, both originally well founded, interpose,
and I see no reason why it should not be left to the free choice of
women, whether they would exercise the political privileges and
follow the pursuits of men. I say left to their free choice, for the
effect of opening the door to all would not necessarily be to entice
all to enter it. Those who had a numerous family would find their
duties at home incompatible with a life abroad. At least this would
be the case until the system had become thoroughly established,
and time and experience suggested many ways of overcoming
difficulties which had not before been thought of. This is a very
common occurrence. Individuals are unexpectedly thrown into
a new situation, and this very circumstance inspires them with
the intelligence and address which are necessary to accommodate
themselves to it. In all probability wherever the husband followed
a trade or profession, the wife would be a partner. Partners in law
or medicine, in commerce, manufactures and the mechanic arts,
&c are now very common. A firm composed of those who were
partners for life, would be the most natural think imaginable. In
this way the husband would be able to relieve the wife when she

was confined at home, as the wife would take the place of the husband when he was absent, or confined by sickness or some other infirmity. With regard to agriculture, which constitutes the pursuit of much the greater part of the population, in every community but Great Britain the ease with which the partnership would be formed is obvious enough. There the house and the farm are the place where the business is transacted: there is no office, or shop abroad, to which it is necessary to repair daily. In many instances I have known men disabled for months, sometimes for years, from actively superintending their affairs, and nothing stood in the way of their wives managing for them, but the fact that it was not the custom, and therefore not proper for them to do so. I have known physicians and lawyers, confined by infirmity for years, so that their business, the sole dependence of their families for subsistence, was entirely destroyed. If public opinion had permitted their wives to be educated as they were, their business would have suffered no interruption and their families would not have been reduced to hopeless poverty.

Secondly, will the indiscriminate association of the sexes encourage a greater degree of licentiousness than now exists? Both Plato and Aristotle have remarked upon the extreme licentiousness of the Spartan women. But two circumstances must be remarked. First, the whole tendency of the Spartan discipline was to produce the deepest corruption in the manners of both men and women. Second, the two sexes were by no means placed upon the same footing. Women were looked upon as possessing a mere animal nature, and as such destined only to rear strong and healthy children for the State. Never was there a society pretending to be civilized, in which care was so industriously taken to degrade the human character. Women were inured to the same sports and exercises as men, and there the equality ceased. There was no education for either sex, no discipline fitted to inspire noble sentiments and to brace the mind against the temptations to which life in its best state is exposed. Women were taught to believe that an animal existence was their sole destination: whereas the true design of placing men and women morally and socially on the same footing is to counteract the strong tendency of our animal nature, to master all the higher faculties; it is to give a direction to the tastes and pursuits of women, which will elevate their character, and by so doing act as a perpetual check upon both their own conduct and on the conduct of men. The principal reason of the wide licentiousness which now exists is that beneath all the refinement and cultivation which adorns the manners, the sentiment is constantly lurking that women have been formed chiefly to gratify the passions of men. The high standard of education which is beginning to be introduced is already operating a change in this respect. The mere seclusion of women, so far from having this effect, acts in a contrary direction. It contributes to pamper and stimulate the passions. There is infinitely more licentiousness of manners in Spain, Portugal and Italy than in the United States or Great Britain, where women have a freer existence, and are placed intellectually more upon a level with men. If we lift still higher their desires and pursuits, their character upon well known principles of human nature will become still more elevated. One idea will no longer reign supreme over the life of women, enfeebling their understandings, and administering constant provocative to the passions of both men and women. The only effectual moral restraint, the only one which can be depended upon to produce genuine integrity of character, is that which is created by education, meaning by education, the entire discipline which pervades the whole of life, not merely the period of youth.

Every one must have remarked the powerful influence which serious occupations have in forming the character to correct and regular habits. Deliver us from ourselves; deliver us from the devouring appetites and propensities which consume life from puberty to the grave, would be the prayer of the wise and the thoughtful. And fortunately the circumstances in which the great majority of men are placed, are such that this end is attained without any set purpose on their part. Man, alone of all animal creation, is obliged to earn his subsistence by toil and labor, and man is the only being who is in danger of being run away with his passions. His craving necessities, and the constant employment to which they goad him, constitute the great balance wheel in his structure, and convert him from a being of instinct and appetites, into one of reflection and reason. In every country the proportion of those who gain their subsistence by some sort of occupation to those who are enabled to live upon an income, is very large, probably nineteen to one, and nearly all of the smaller number have previously accumulated the capital from which their revenue is derived, by some kind of business. Labor which has been regarded as a curse has proved itself a blessing, for it contributes more than all the positive institutions of society, to the happiness and well being of the community.

If women then are introduced into the engrossing occupations of life, the effect will be highly salutary. The habits of industry, reflection, and self-reliance which will be created, will act as a counterpoise to the licentiousness which would otherwise take place. The circle of their ideas will be enlarged, greater vigor of character will be acquired, and a consequence there will be a firmer and a more general reliance upon themselves for the establishment of a reputation. The more the responsibility of our actions is cast upon us, the stronger is the sense of that responsibility. Third, will the perfect equality of man and wife, mar the tranquility of domestic life? Unity of counsel and unity of action are as necessary in the family as in the affairs of government. Will this be frustrated by placing men and women on an equal footing? The decided elevation of women and children, at the present day, has really contributed more than any other circumstance to domestic harmony. The free institutions of the United States, combined with the improved system of education which is adopted, have produced the result. Innumerable checks are thus place upon the conduct of husbands, wives and children. These are unseen and unfelt, and even agreeable in their influence. The same effect has been wrought in the family as has been produced in the state, by lifting the people to a higher condition. It was predicted in Great Britain, when this new power was created to thwart the purposes of the crown and aristocracy, that the whole plan of government would lose the character of unity which was before impressed upon it. The reverse is the case: there is more singleness of purpose discernible in all the acts of the government because their interests are more identical than was ever before known. Unity of action is sought through diversity of counsel, and the more elevated the condition of those who participate in both, the happier will be the result.

I have observed that husband and will often be partners in the occupation which is followed for the maintenance of the family. They will be partners in a profession, or in one or other of the great departments of industry: and this identity of pursuits conspiring with an identity of interests, will contribute to render the path of life easier, and more agreeable. To think alike with regard to the commonwealth has always been looked upon as forming a strong bond of connection in public life. To think alike with regard to any subject which is of magnitude sufficient to engross the affections has the same effect, and more especially is it so, as between the two who are not united by a temporary interest, but who are embarked for life in the pursuit of a common end. Perhaps all the objects of human pursuit would sink into insignificance, if looked down upon by a superior being. Perhaps this is the sentiment of all in the hour of death. But as we cannot clothe ourselves with a nature superior to that with which we were born, nor always possess the wisdom, or the weakness of a dying man, we must make the best of things as they are, and endeavor so to mold the materials which are placed at our command, as to extract from them the greatest amount of good.

I have avoided all detail in this examination. I have omitted a great many views which suggest themselves in answer to difficulties. I have studied brevity and concision, as I am writing an essay, not a volume. As Des Cartes said, all he desired was that the reader should imitate his method, so all I desire is that the reader will follow the vigorous analysis I have observed. It may be the means of conducting him to the truth, on whichever side it lies.

Four Grimke Siblings:
Finding their Places in Life

Comprised of approximately two thousand items, the University of Michigan Clements Library's Weld-Grimké archive has been used extensively by women's studies scholars as a comprehensive, though not complete, record of the sisters' private lives and public careers. The archive's holdings that directly concern Frederick are much more limited, and consist almost entirely of his letters to Sarah. But for scholars interested in his life and works it has provided, as one of them has said with some exaggeration, "most of what one can discover" about him.[25] Practically all the archive's materials are manuscripts, and some of the handwriting is difficult to decipher. With no detailed index or electronically searchable transcriptions, it is not easy to find everything relevant to a particular research interest, and spending additional effort to investigate something not obviously germane, initially noticed as a mere curiosity, would not be enticing to researchers working under time constraints imposed by the urgency of completing a project, or the duration of a planned visit to Ann Arbor.

It is thus not surprising that, of the users of the Weld-Grimké archive, scholars interested in Frederick's life and works make, in their writings, no significant mention of the sisters; and scholars interested in the sisters' lives and works make, in their writings (with one exception) no significant mention of Frederick.[26] As a result (even in the excepted instance, recounted below) they have bypassed matters of importance to their respective topics, particularly as to sibling relationships. Despite age differences extending over a span of nineteen years, four of the Grimké family members demonstrate what Lorri Glover and other scholars have identified as a "powerful component of early American family life: the ease and mutuality of sibling relations" established as members of the same generation drew on each other for attention and support.[27]

The phenomenon has been marked as particularly noteworthy in relations between siblings of opposite sex. Although, as Glover states, there were "highly gendered guidelines for appropriate behavior within the patriarchial family" in husband-wife and parent-child relations, "brothers and sisters escaped this and remained free to construct relationships as they saw fit."[28] As in other families, Grimké sibling relationships were both varied in intensity, and intermittent. But among these four they were unusually powerful. For Sarah and Thomas in childhood, for the sisters with each other in their entire lives, for the sisters and Thomas as adults, and for the sisters – especially Sarah – and Frederick in mature life, sibling relationships were remarkably productive of intellectual development, creative thought, and social action.

- - - -

Born in 1791 and 1792 into a distinguished South Carolina family, Frederick and Sarah were respectively the fifth and sixth of fourteen Grimké children. Their father John Faucheraud Grimké, had been sent to England as a youth, to be educated at Cambridge and the Middle Temple. He returned to serve in the Revolutionary army, succeeded to his inheritance as a plantation owner, and became a South Carolina appellate court judge. His wife, Mary Smith Grimké came from a family no less prominent in Charleston

society. Their second child Thomas, an older brother to Frederick
and Sarah, was born in 1786; their fourteenth child, Angelina was
born in 1805. Thomas and Frederick were sent north to college,
both to Yale, where Frederick graduated in 1810, a few months short
of his nineteenth birthday.

Neither Sarah nor Angelina had any institutional education.
From Thomas's youthful willingness to share his lessons Sarah
gained childhood opportunities, unusual then for girls, to learn
something of mathematics, geography, world history, Greek,
natural science and botany. But their father Judge Grimké drew the
line at her joining in Thomas's studies of Latin – a disappointment
she would bitterly recall in later life.[29] Competence in Latin was a
Yale admissions requirement, typically met with the aid of tutoring,
and if that was Thomas's situation when Judge Grimké frustrated
Sarah's aspiration to join her brother in learning the language, it
would have occurred around 1803 when Thomas was seventeen and
she was eleven. Sarah idolized Thomas.

She did not have that feeling for Frederick during their
childhood years. Five years younger than Thomas but only a year
older than Sarah, he might have been a rival, not a mentor in her
childhood quest for education. That he is not mentioned in any of
her early life memoirs is consistent with what could be surmised
from retrospective projection of Frederick's adult personality – that
he was self-absorbed, awkward, and socially immature. He entered
Yale at age fifteen, two years younger than Thomas had been on
his first arriving in New Haven.

Thomas and Frederick:
Early Nineteenth-Century Yale and Women's Rights

Under the presidencies of Ezra Stiles (1778 to 1795) and Timothy Dwight (1795 to 1817) Yale evolved from a "collegiate school" for training Connecticut clergymen and schoolmasters to an institution of higher learning with a nationwide constituency and a mission to prepare its sons for leadership in the life of the new nation. Changes in the college curriculum reflected this transformation. Both Stiles and Dwight conducted regular debating exercises for seniors, on questions which included issues of political and social significance. For the most part these exercises were "forensic disputations" in which students delivered oral presentations of previously written-out arguments. Each debate was followed by extensive comments from Stiles or Dwight explaining their judgment of the merits of the question, and addressing only incidentally, if at all, the debaters' forensic skills.[30] Similar exercises for underclassmen were conducted by the college's tutors – junior faculty members, who were recent graduates. And Yale students themselves, who as the late Professor Edmund Morgan wrote, "could never get enough of the interminable ceremonial talking," chose many of the questions debated in academic exercises, to revisit in their own "literary societies."[31]

These were remarkable organizations. Besides maintaining a library of books purchased with membership dues, each society had its own extensive program of oratory and debate in which all members participated. Two such organizations that thrived when the Grimké brothers were at Yale – Linonia, to which they both belonged, and another called Brothers in Unity – had memberships which together included virtually all undergraduates. Meeting weekly and with members taking part in rotation, the Yale societies provided students with forensic experiences greater in variety, broader in topical content, and more inclusive in extent of student participation than are found there, or on any other U.S. college campus, today. Another Yale historian has described the literary societies' activities as being "among the most potent factors of [Yale's] influence in the first half of the nineteenth century."[32] Both Grimké brothers experienced that influence. Describing it in a speech, "The Importance of the Art of Speaking, and of Debating Societies," given in Charleston more than two decades after his graduation, Thomas recalled being told by his tutor "that if a young man were obliged to neglect either his College studies, or the exercises of his Society, to slight the former would be preferred in the long run" – to which, after recounting the remark in his speech, Thomas simply added, "I say the same."[33]

In addition to issues of current topical interest (in June, 1787, for example, Stiles had his students debate whether the states had "acted wisely" in sending delegates to the Convention in Philadelphia, and in November of that year, whether the Constitution they framed should be ratified), were questions set in eternal or indefinite time frames (*e.g.* "Is a lie ever justifiable?" "Would a permanent Navy be beneficial to the United States?").[34] Many of the questions initially raised in disputations the college presidents conducted for seniors were taken up by the tutors in exercises for underclassmen, and revisited by students in literary society debates, becoming perennial topics argued over and over without deference to previous rulings on the merits. Society debate records are remarkably extensive, and in tracing students' individual participation it is intriguing to find encounters with issues some would meet again, in later life. For the Grimké brothers there were two such issues, not as yet much deliberated in the nation at large but already of long standing at Yale. Slavery was one of the issues. The other was the status and role of women in American society.

In 1771, seven years before becoming Yale's president and while he was a Congregational minister in Newport, Rhode Island, Ezra Stiles recorded in his diary a conversation with a deacon in the local Baptist church, concerning women church members deliberating and voting on matters that came before Baptist congregations for disposition. "On the whole," Stiles wrote, "it appears to me that there is a Usage and practiced Principle among the Baptists of this Colony to admit the Sisters to equal Votes in the Chh [church] meetings." As to what women members actually did in the meetings, Stiles distinguished a growing custom to "keep their places and say nothing" from active participation in deliberations, where women members' votes might be decisive. He found the latter practice to be rare among the Baptists, and in decline. Comparing churches of his own Congregational denomination he went on to note, "I never knew or read of the Sisters voting" even on admission of new members, which required unanimous consent. That troubled him, for, as he wrote, "upon the principle that there can be no vote [to admit] unless every Brother consented, the Consent of every Sister may be required." He thought that males who supported the mandate for unanimity while denying the vote to women spoke "inconsistently."[35]

In 1782, after Stiles had become Yale's president and doubled the time undergraduates spent on forensic exercises, he began to assign "Whether female Academies would be beneficial?" and

"Whether Females ought to be admitted to public civil government?" for argument in disputations he conducted.[36] An extraordinary encounter the following year would intensify his interest in female education. In December, 1783, Stiles met twelve year old Lucinda Foote, a minister's daughter, and having examined her on readings of Greek and Roman texts he awarded her a formally captioned "Certificate or Diploma on Parchment," signed by him as president of Yale, attesting to his finding (as here translated from Latin) that "she has made commendable progress, giving the true meaning of passages in the Aeneid of Virgil, the Select Orations of Cicero, and in the Greek Testament; *and that she is fully qualified, except in regard to sex, to be received as a pupil in the Freshman Class of Yale College* [italics added]."[37] Stiles recorded the text of the instrument in his diary entry of December 22, 1783.

That was almost two centuries before Yale would admit women as undergraduates. But Yale students of the time had already found the subject intriguing. Minutes of spring, 1788 meetings of both literary societies – among the earliest such records which survive – indicate that by then the question of women in government was being chosen for argument. In August, 1793, Stiles read Mary Wollstonecraft's *Vindication of the Rights of Woman*, probably at the instance of an acquaintance just returned from London, who had met her there, and whose account of her personal life interested Stiles enough to read the work and record the experience in his diary. She did not argue for women's participation in business, the professions, or government service. Rather, it was for "dignified domestic happiness" in middle age, after the physical "person of a woman is no longer preferred to her mind," that Wollstonecraft was inspired to add female education to a scheme

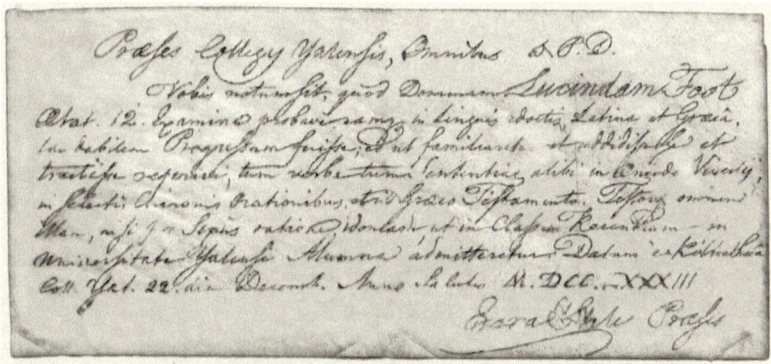

Illustration 3. "Certificate or Diploma on Parchment," issued by Yale President Ezra Stiles to Lucinda Foote, Dec. 22, 1783. Manuscripts and Archives, Yale University Library

Latin Text

(L.S.) Praeses Collegij Yalensis, Omnibus S. P. D.
Vobis notum sit quod Dominum

Lucindam Foot. Aetat 12. Examine probavi, eamque in Linguis edoctis, Latina et Graeca, laudabilem progressum fecisse; eo ut familiariter et reddidisse & tractasse reperivi, tum verba tum Sententias, alibi in Aeneide Virgilii, in selectis Ciceronis Orationibus, et in Graeco Testamento. Testorque omnino illam, nisi Sexus ratione, idoneam ut in Classem Recentium in Universitate Yalensi Alumna admitteretur. Datum e Bibliotheca Collegij Yalensis, 22 die Decembris, Anno Salutis MDCCLXXXIII.

Ezra Stiles, Praeses

English Translation

The President of Yale College, to all to whom these Presents

Shall Come – Greeting

Be it known to you, that I have examined Miss Lucinda Foote, twelve years old, and have found that in the learned languages – the Latin and the Greek – she has made commendable progress, giving the true meaning of passages in the Aeneid of Virgil, the Select Orations of Cicero, and in the Greek Testament; and that she is fully qualified, except in regard to sex, to be received as a pupil in the Freshman Class of Yale College. Given at the Library, Yale College, December 22, 1783.

Ezra Stiles, President

"THE UNSOLVED PROBLEM."

Shall the weaker and downtrodden sex receive shelter in our cloisters?

Illustration 4. The Unsolved Problem, drawing in the *Yale Banner* college yearbook (1872), on an unnumbered page which follows p. 32.

The drawing has no accompanying text, but students would have connected it with an inquiry as to whether a female might be permitted to attend the law school, which Yale president Noah Porter (the drawing's perplexed male subject) referred to the university's governing board. The response was negative. See Judith Ann Schiff, "Yale's First Female Graduate," *Yale Alumni Magazine,* Sept./Oct. 2013.

Talleyrand had advocated in a work published in 1791, early in the course of the French Revolution.[38] Stiles's reading and re-reading of Wollstonecraft's book is mentioned in four of his daily diary entries.[39] Less than a year later, by remarkable happenstance, he met Talleyrand during the latter's sojourn in the U.S. after being expelled from England, where he had taken refuge when the French National Convention ordered his arrest. Stiles's diary account of their meeting indicates that they discussed the situation of childhood education in New England. Wollstonecraft's dedication of her book to Talleyrand – something Stiles had previously noted in his diary – suggests that their conversation might have touched on improved educational opportunities for girls or women.[40] Indeed it might well have, for by that time the topic was a familiar topic of discourse on the Yale campus. Talleyrand's visit on July 17, 1794 was less than three weeks after "Ought the education of females to be more assimilated to that of the males?" was argued by members of the college chapter of Phi Beta Kappa. The Linonians argued the same question two weeks later. "Whether women ought to be admitted to a share in civil government?" had been a Brothers in Unity debate topic two years before, on July 19, 1792.[41]

Stiles's successor Timothy Dwight had once taught in a coeducational grammar school in Northampton, Massachusetts. In 1795 "Female Education" was the topic of the English Oration at the first college commencement over which he presided, and he would soon add women's intellectual capacity as a subject of disputations he conducted.[42] In 1796, when he assigned "Whether the mental abilities of females are equal to that of the males?" one of his students stayed up late to prepare his argument "in the affirmative

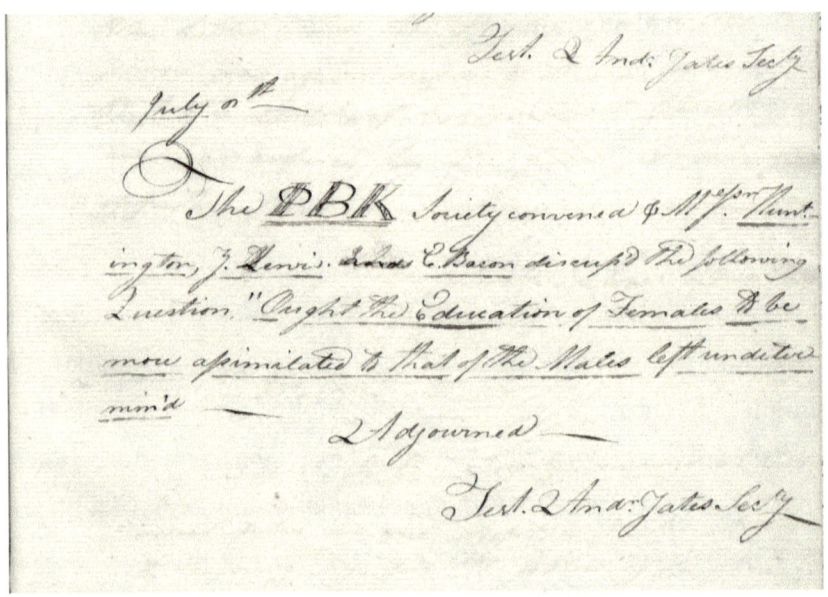

Illustration 5. Phi Beta Kappa Society, Yale Chapter Minutes, Jul. 1, 1794. Manuscripts and Archives, Yale University Library

of which I am a strenuous advocate," noting in his diary that the question was "warmly contested at the eleven o'clock recitation, and decided in favor of the females, after a debate of more than two hours."[43] That student, Benjamin Silliman, Sr., would subsequently have a distinguished scientific career as a member of the Yale faculty.

Dwight would make a more qualified judgment of the same question when it was argued before him in another disputation seventeen years later. He then held that "there can be no decision on this subject, because the different manner of education of the different sexes deprives us of the facts." But his assessment of how women stood in respect to that difference was incisive: "it is," he told his students, "owing [only] to the good sense of the women of this country, that they are not absolute idiots." This judgment is recorded in notes of Dwight's rulings on questions in disputations he conducted during the 1814-15 academic year, for a senior class of which his son Theodore, who took the notes, was a member. When the younger Dwight came to publish them in 1833 he explained that he had noted under the heading "Remarks" comments his father made during the course of the argument, as distinct from the "Decision," Dwight's ruling given at the conclusion of the exercise. Both are included in the text here re-published in Appendix A.

For Yale students "equal ability" of the sexes became a regular topic of debating activities both in their literary societies and in Phi Beta Kappa chapter meetings, during Dwight's presidency. It was chosen as a topic for public exhibitions of disputation and oratory that were part of college graduation exercises, and it was undoubtedly a frequent subject of conversation among students, and with their tutors – in Frederick's case with his tutor Sereno Dwight, another of President Dwight's sons.[44] It is thus practically certain that every Yale student of Thomas and Frederick's time was at least familiar with, if he did not personally engage in, considered arguments on women's equality in intellectual capacity, and potential to benefit from higher education.

Literary society members took turns as advocates in disputations, and rotated frequently in and out of their organizations' presidencies and other offices. Like Stiles and Dwight for the disputations they conducted as faulty members, the societies' student presidents passed on the merits of questions argued before them. Their judgments in debates were usually recorded only summarily in the secretary's minutes (*e.g.* "decided in the affirmative," along with the question debated, the advocates' names, and the sides for which they argued). But Frederick's decisions on topics he heard argued while serving as Linonia's president were reported descriptively, and reflect his taking his judicial responsibilities seriously. Of his decision of the first such question – "Ought the debtor to be imprisoned at the will of the creditor?" – the secretary wrote, "Mr. Grimke, the president, gave a handsome decision in the negative." On another question, "Is the study of dead languages beneficial?" Frederick's negative ruling was complimented as "judicious." And in a debate as to whether students "destined to different professions" should be offered "different courses of study" in college, he delivered "a few remarks, but did not attempt a decision."[45]

Frederick missed Linonia's July 4, 1810 meeting at which "Are the abilities of the sexes equal?" was argued before a small turnout of the few members who were not otherwise occupied that evening, probably celebrating the national holiday. But a few weeks later, after his graduation, the Linonians debated another issue he would confront in mature life. Having remained in New Haven that summer, Frederick and another classmate were invited by students who were still active members of the society to attend its next debate and offer remarks following arguments by the regularly appointed advocates. The question was "Ought the slaves in the United States [to] be immediately emancipated?" "The dispute was ably and warmly conducted by both sides," the secretary reported, and "all engagements were punctually fulfilled; the meeting was, for the time of year, uncommonly full, decorum and strict attention [were] observed." Frederick spoke for the negative.[46]

Thomas, Frederick, Sarah and Angelina:
Growing Up and Leaving Home

Thomas had less time for Sarah when he returned to Charleston after graduating in the Class of 1807. Inspired by Yale's president Timothy Dwight, whom he had accompanied on travels during a college summer vacation, he was at first eager for a life in the ministry. Judge Grimké, disapproving, redirected his aspirations to a career in law, but that did not dampen Thomas's enthusiasm for inspirational speech and idealistic causes. In 1809, the year of his admission to the bar, he delivered and published his first lecture, on "the character of an accomplished orator." In another lecture that year, a July 4th oration, he argued for maintaining strong bonds of national union.[47] Years later during the Nullification crisis he would contend again for that cause in the most famous of his cases in the South Carolina courts, *M'Cready v. Hunt* (1834), disputing the constitutionality of an oath required of state militiamen that implied supremacy of state over federal law.[48] Meanwhile, in 1810 Thomas had married; in 1826 he was elected to the state senate; and in 1832, after he had acquired a national reputation for eloquently expressed but not widely accepted positions in support of temperance, pacifism, state-law codification, simplified spelling, and reform of grammar school education, Yale awarded him an honorary doctor of laws degree.

Frederick, by contrast, was introverted and retiring, and little is known of his life in Charleston after returning there from college in 1810. He was admitted to the South Carolina bar but appears to have had no significant practice. A case for which his participation is mentioned in family memoirs was a politically inspired impeachment prosecution brought in 1811 against his father, Judge Grimké, in which Frederick and Thomas both assisted a more senior lawyer in securing an acquittal. In 1818 Frederick left his native city and state, never to return. None of his writings expresses any reason for his departure. A scholar who has written about his works, Maxwell Bloomfield, suggests that escape from the aura of Thomas's celebrity weighed heavily in his decision to make his life elsewhere.[49] But Frederick was not envious or resentful of his brother, and they were never on bad terms.

Nor is there anything to account for his choice to emigrate to Ohio. After first settling in Columbus, newly established out of the wilderness as the permanent state capital, he moved thirty miles south to spend the rest of his life in Chillicothe. With a population largely southern in origin and outlook and a political heritage derived from its prominence as the first state capital, the town well suited Frederick. A modest law practice brought recognition of his intellectual acuity, which soon gained him a seat on the common pleas bench. He never married, and never owned a house, preferring to live as a boarder in what were euphemistically called "hotels." Eccentricities including extreme fastidiousness (he engaged the town barber for an hour each morning to dress and groom him), and especially his awkwardness in the company of women, amused Chillicotheans. No picture of him is known to exist apart from portraits fellow townsmen painted in words. One writer of local history described him as thin and angular in physique, his "eyes, black and overhung with heavy gray and black brows," his "nose thin and aquiline," and recalled his habit of "taking long and rapid walks, or rides on horseback, always alone."[50] Another recounted her vivid childhood memory of seeing

Frederick dressed in a swallow-tail coat with "a white neck cloth [which] encircled his throat in voluminous folds, the ends tied in a precise little bow," standing with "gloved hands held stiffly straight to his sides," touching "strapped pantaloons guiltless of crease or wrinkles," all with an appearance "so stiff, so mechanical, as to resemble one of those figures whose jerky motions are governed by machinery."[51] But if he was socially awkward he was not disagreeable or quarrelsome. No one who served as an Ohio lawyer or judge when Frederick did, could have failed to possess the companionability requisite for members of a frontier bench and bar as they rode, worked, and lived together for weeks at a time, sharing the poor meals and primitive accommodations of professional life on the state's early judicial circuits.

Sarah's transition to womanhood was burdened with frustration, as she successively embraced roles into which she did not quite fit. Twelve and a half when Angelina was born in 1805, she became a surrogate mother to this youngest sister, even seeking and being given permission to stand as Angelina's godmother. In 1809, at age seventeen, Sarah came out in Charleston society to engage for the next two years in the social life which for young women of her station was a prelude to marriage. She had one suitor, broke off, and came to think of herself as unattractive. An 1812 encounter with a Presbyterian minister (the Grimkés were Episcopalians) led to an intense spiritual experience of charitable work and self-denial, lasting several years. In 1819 she was called to a difficult service of filial devotion when her father, whose health had deteriorated since his impeachment trial, decided to travel north to consult a noted Philadelphia physician, and chose Sarah to be his companion and caregiver on the journey. She performed that mission capably,

lovingly, and selflessly. After two months of treatment that brought
no improvement the doctor recommended a therapeutic sojourn
on the New Jersey shore, where John Faucheraud Grimké died on
August 8, 1819. Sarah had to arrange for last rites and a burial that
no other family member could attend.

A prominent Quaker whom she met as a fellow passenger
on the voyage back to Charleston inspired her attraction to the
religious life of that sect, which, after several return visits to
Philadelphia, Sarah joined as a member of the city's congregation.
Recounted in detail in Mark Perry's history of the Grimké family,
her Philadelphia visits alternated with unhappy sojourns back in
Charleston, each of several months. Her mother Mary Grimké
had great difficulty accepting Sarah's adoption of Quaker dress
and mannerisms, and resented Sarah's objection to her claiming
the perquisites of dowager life in southern planter society. With
Thomas, on the other hand, Sarah remained on good terms despite
their disagreement over a new topic of discussion: how slavery,
which both regarded as an evil, should be remediated. Thomas
advocated resettlement out of the U.S. by induced colonization;
Sarah insisted on abolition.[52]

A teenager nearly fifteen when Sarah returned to Charleston
after their father's death, Angelina continued to look to her for
sympathy and support. Maintaining her childhood custom of
addressing Sarah as "mother" while frequently in conflict with
their birth mother, Angelina joined Sarah in rejecting the family's
Episcopalian religious heritage and subsequently in adopting
Quakerism. But as Mark Perry perceptively notes, the two sisters "in
fact looked at the world rather differently." Sarah was emotional, he
wrote, "whereas Angelina showed extraordinary calm; Sarah was

haunted by self-doubt and feelings of inadequacy, whereas Angelina was self-confident, rebellious and strong-willed." These differences would persist, establishing a "pattern of their collaboration" which became evident later, in public life. "In time," as Perry succinctly put it, "Sarah Grimké would be acknowledged as one of the leading reform thinkers of her age, but her sister Angelina would always be remembered as a crusader."[53]

In 1829, the year after Angelina's conversion to Quakerism, she went to live with Sarah and joined the Quaker community in Philadelphia. Each was uncomfortable in that affiliation – Angelina with her less than complete acceptance of tenets of the Quaker faith, Sarah, a poor speaker, with her failure to meet expectations of articulate participation in Quaker meetings. Both were troubled by the absence of a Quaker doctrinal position against slavery, but they did not give voice to this concern. For the next five years the sisters devoted themselves to acceptance of religious life within the Philadelphia Quaker community, avoiding involvement in disagreements among its members as to how slavery should be ended in the United States.

Thomas's Loss: a Transformative Event

In 1834 the Grimké family suffered a tragedy, with consequences not fully perceived by historians for whom Frederick, on the one hand, and Sarah and Angelina, on the other, have separately become subjects of interest. Having accepted invitations for two speaking engagements in Ohio – one from the Eurodephians, a Miami University student literary society, the other from the

Western Literary Society and College of Professional Teachers in Cincinnati – Thomas embarked on a trip north. He planned it to begin with a visit to the sisters in Philadelphia and, after the speaking appearances, to end with a week spent with Frederick in central Ohio. For a time all went well. A happy reunion with Sarah and Angelina in a September visit lasting several days provided an exciting opportunity to exchange views on slavery, a subject on which Thomas promised to reexamine his position (he had earlier favored transportation of the slaves out of the country and resettlement elsewhere). He also showed the sisters an essay he had written, on women's education. Angelina copied that work, making an extra copy for Thomas to take with him.

His visit to Miami University in Oxford, Ohio was a triumph; for his lecture "The Comparative Eloquence of Ancient and Modern Times" Thomas was lionized by the students, and had his portrait painted. In Cincinnati his topic was "American Education." And it was probably there that he contracted the disease which struck him suddenly on October 12, 1834 on his way to meet Frederick in Columbus. Critically ill when he was taken off the stagecoach a few miles short of that destination, he died within hours of cholera.

Thomas's death hit the sisters especially hard. Their first response beyond private grief was to compose a memorial, "A Sketch of Thomas Grimké's Life Written by his Sisters in Philadelphia and Sent to his Friends in Charleston," which they subsequently had published in a journal of the American Peace Society.[54] The sisters and Frederick each saw to publication of works Thomas had left in manuscript. Frederick arranged this for his two Ohio lectures, and sent back to Angelina the copy she had made of Thomas's essay on education. Angelina, or both sisters, then submitted the essay for publication in a newspaper. The clipping from one of its columns now found in the Weld-Grimké archive's miscellany does not identify the paper, but a January, 1836 publication date may be inferred from a reverse-side news report of Congressional proceedings known to have occurred early that month.[55]

For the sisters, Thomas's achievements of translating privately held ideals into publicly advocated causes became an inspiration and a mandate. Catherine Birney, who knew Sarah well and was her first biographer, recalled that "the loss of her brother almost crushed Sarah," but that "later, in the early part of 1835, after having re-perused her brother's works, she solemnly dedicated herself to the cause of peace, persuading herself that Thomas had left it as a legacy to her and Angelina."[56] "We often conversed on the subject of slavery . . . [but] God took him away," Sarah wrote in 1838 to Theodore Weld, one of William Lloyd Garrison's lieutenants in the abolitionist movement. "My own views were dark and confused," she continued. "Had I my present light, I might have helped him."[57] "He was deeply interested in *every* reform," Angelina would write years later, "and saw very clearly that the anti-slavery agitation which began in 1832 would shake our country to its foundation. He told me in Philadelphia that he knew slavery would be the all-absorbing subject here, and that he intended to devote a whole year to its investigation."[58] But Angelina must also have realized that Thomas's making a public declaration for abolition while he and his family lived in Charleston would have branded him as an outcast, and put even his life in peril. Opposition to Nullification had already brought threats to his personal safety.[59] So it is not surprising that Angelina, always given to action, would take it for both of them. In September, 1835, less than a year after Thomas's death, her letter denouncing slavery was published in *The Liberator* with an introduction by its editor, William Lloyd Garrison, identifying Angelina as Thomas's sister.[60] In October, 1836 she published her *Appeal to the Christian Women of the Southern States.* Two months after that Sarah followed with her first anti-slavery work, *Epistle to the Clergy of the Southern States.*[61]

With these actions the sisters' lives were transformed. For the next two years until Angelina's marriage to Weld in 1838, they were active as publicists for emancipation and women's rights. Discountenanced by the Philadelphia Quakers, these activities effectively ended the sisters' membership in that community. In May, 1837 they began a New England speaking tour. Angelina's appearance before a committee of the Massachusetts legislature, along with a group of New England clergymen's widely publicized disapproval of her and Sarah's addressing "promiscuous" (*i.e.* mixed gender) audiences, energized the sisters' commitment to the feminist movement, a cause they viewed as closely related to abolition of slavery. "It was when my soul was deeply moved at the wrongs of the slave that I first perceived distinctly the abject condition of women," Sarah wrote. "It requires but little thought to see that the conditions of women and that of slaves are in many respects parallel."[62] "We are willing to bear the brunt of the storm," Angelina declared in a letter written in 1837, "if we can only be the means of making a break in that wall of public opinion which lies right in the way of women's rights, true dignity, honor and usefulness."[63]

Sarah came out in 1838 with her *Letters on the Equality of the Sexes and the Condition of Women,* a foundation work of American feminist thought.[64] "In examining this important subject," she declared in Letter I, "I shall depend solely on the Bible to designate the sphere of woman."[65] Her first published observations on the extent of that "sphere" in respect to American women's education and remunerative work outside the home are in Letter VIII, "On the Condition of Women in the United States." Here Sarah quoted a passage from Thomas's essay on women's education, attributing it to "a late American writer" identified by name in a footnote. But her quotation had an omission.

Appendix B, which here sets forth Thomas's essay in its entirety, highlights words which Sarah, quoting it in her Letter VIII, left out. Thomas did not consider the purposes of giving women "an approach to the best education now given to men" to include enabling women to engage in occupations outside the home for which higher education was requisite. Thus he would not have had women instructed in subjects "perfectly manly, such as public speaking and political studies, or purely professional, as Law, Medicine, and Divinity." It was the expression of this exception that Sarah omitted, without comment, and without disclosing the omission to her readers. But whether that may be taken to imply a claim for women's participation in occupations Thomas had reserved as "perfectly manly," may be doubted. It seems more likely that Sarah had not yet given the question much thought. "All I complain of," she wrote "is, that our education consists so almost exclusively in culinary and manual operations." Sarah wanted to see husbands "encourage their wives to devote some portion of their time to mental cultivation, even at the expense of having to dine sometimes on baked potatoes, or bread and butter."[66] She went on in the same Letter VIII to lament the low wages being paid for unskilled work performed by working-class women, citing the importance of their earnings as household income. In Letter XIV she claimed an equal right for women to preach on matters of faith, but she did not advocate their engaging in the ministry as a profession. Nowhere in her *Letters on the Equality of the Sexes* did Sarah assert any connection between higher education for women and careers in the professional or commercial workplaces for which such education is requisite.

In May, 1838, during the week after Angelina's marriage to Theodore Weld, a public meeting the sisters addressed was broken up by hecklers, and that night the Philadelphia meeting hall where they spoke was burned down by a mob. Shocked and unnerved by this violence, they withdrew from public life. The Welds invited Sarah to make her home with them as they came to live in New Jersey in places not far from New York City: first in Ft. Lee, then near Belleville, where Sarah helped them purchase a farm. There they lived a hard life on a meager income, Theodore Weld having to support his parents who resided nearby, Angelina sickly and depending on Sarah for the care of the three Weld children, and Sarah becoming their surrogate mother as she once had been Angelina's.

Meanwhile, in 1836, Frederick had been promoted to the Ohio Supreme Court to sit as one of its four judges, all elected by the legislature. The court was an itinerant tribunal, required by the state constitution to hold annual sessions in each of Ohio's then some seventy counties. Even with the state divided into two judicial circuits to enable sessions to be conducted by two-judge panels, the requirement for each judge's sitting in half the state's counties together with attending a two or three week session of the full court held once a year in Columbus, imposed extraordinary demands for official travel, almost all of it on horseback. As one of Frederick's judicial colleagues counted it up, it amounted to an astounding 2,250 miles per year.[67] Opinion writing – Frederick's were learned and lengthy – took another considerable portion of his time.[68] So it is not surprising that during these years of his judicial service, before the advent of rail travel, he made no visits to his sisters back east.

Lives Unfulfilled: Frederick's Abbreviated Judicial Career; Sarah's "Disciplinary Circumstances"

Frederick resigned from the Ohio Supreme Court in 1842, a year short of completing his seven-year term, and thereafter had no further judicial service or active engagement in the practice of law. He left no explanation of why he left the legal profession. If hard conditions of circuit life had something to do with it, he had at least endured them for over twenty years, and there is no indication of any decline in his health. Supported by a small income from his father's estate and continuing to reside in Chillicothe, he gave his full time to pursuit of intellectual interests in political theory. His treatise, *Considerations Upon the Nature and Tendency of Free Institutions*, was published in a first edition in 1848.

In that same year the Welds turned their Belleville farm into a small coeducational boarding school, in which Sarah taught French and shared the work of operation.[69] Five years later, in 1853, the Welds encountered a better prospect for maintaining their financial well-being when leaders of the Raritan Bay Union invited them to join their newly established cooperative living community,

"Eagleswood," and take over operation of its school. Located near Perth Amboy, New Jersey, Eagleswood was one of several such ventures in the United States inspired by the teachings of French social theorist Francois Fourier. Sarah subsidized the Welds' move there, using part of an inheritance from her father to purchase stock in the cooperative.

But by then her situation in the Weld household had become unhappy. Angelina was uncomfortable with her and Theodore's dependence on the income Sarah provided from her inheritance to help meet their household expenses, and resented Sarah's mothering of her children. Sarah, on her part, disliked teaching, and was fatigued by having to take a larger share of child care and housework as a result of Angelina's frequent bouts of illness.[70] Tired, depressed, feeling personally unfulfilled and unfairly used, Sarah still did not give in to despair. Writing in March, 1853 to her friend Harriot Hunt she portrayed herself as a "seed cast into the ground," awaiting a time when "the disciplinary circumstances by which [I am] surrounded" would come to provide "nourishment."[71]

Thus, like Frederick a decade earlier, Sarah left a situation with which she was dissatisfied to find a more fulfilling life in the service of her own, deeply held interests and aspirations. She did not find that life immediately. At first she traveled to Philadelphia, then to Washington and Boston, with vaguely formed thoughts of becoming a lawyer or a physician.[72] With no prospect for entering either profession at her age of 61, she rejoined the Welds in 1854, accepting with equanimity the burdens of sharing their life in Eagleswood, but finding time, nevertheless, for a productive second career in the women's rights movement. It was during the next three or four years that she wrote the texts which Elizabeth Bartlett and Gerda Lerner have published as "essays," while maintaining an extensive correspondence and stimulating personal contacts with many of the movement's leaders. Among the visitors Sarah welcomed to Eagleswood were Elizabeth Cady Stanton and others in its next generation of women's rights activists, as well some of the movement's sympathizers, notably Horace Greeley, editor of the New York *Tribune*.[73] Nourished by the same "disciplinary circumstances" which had earlier caused her such unhappiness and frustration, Sarah's "seed cast into the ground" began to grow.

It was not mere coincidence that during the same period she and Frederick came into close personal and intellectual contact. He had managed to make two earlier visits to the sisters in Belleville, one in 1845, the other 1851, of which brief references in letters establishing the approximate dates are all that is known.[74] Beginning in 1854 his visits to Eagleswood were frequent, occurring almost annually, and he and Sarah filled the intervals with articulate and intellectually stimulating correspondence.

A Remarkable Intellectual Collaboration

Frederick and Sarah in the 1850's

Concluding her double biography, *The Grimké Sisters from South Carolina,* with brief portrayals of other Grimké family members' later-life ties with Sarah and Angelina, Professor Gerda Lerner wrote in a paragraph devoted to Frederick, that:

> Judge Grimké was one of the foremost opponents of organized abolitionism, which he had attacked in his book . . . Sarah began to interest her brother in woman's rights. She sent him the proceedings of various conventions, her own and Angelina's writings on the subject, and asked his advice on various points of law. Judge Grimké, in voluminous and tediously dull letters, enlightened Sarah with his legal opinions and otherwise confined his discussion to the Graham diet, the only other interest he shared with his sisters. But the correspondence led to a renewal of family ties; Judge Grimké once even visited the Welds.[75]

As to Frederick, almost none of these assertions is strictly accurate. In his treatise he deplored the forcible importation of African peoples into the American South as slaves, but, that having occurred, he argued that their condition would not be improved by immediate action to render them legally free.[76] He did not otherwise confront supporters of abolition, or directly oppose their activity as an organized movement. His letters to Sarah provided legal advice on her personal affairs: financial assistance to a relative back in Charleston, an inheritance from a deceased brother's estate, security for money due her from a sale of her interest in the Belleville property, gifts she contemplated making in her will, and formal requirements for the will's execution.[77] One doubts that Sarah found any of this advice either tedious or dull. Nor do Frederick's letters mention the Graham diet. It was followed in the Weld household, but the dietary interest he shared with Sarah was in eating moderately.[78]

More significantly, his visits to Sarah and the Welds after they moved to Eagleswood occurred considerably more often than Professor Lerner's "once." "I have been to New Jersey every year," he wrote to Sarah in March, 1858. That was essentially true, for starting in 1854 his visits took place almost yearly – a remarkable frequency considering the distance and hardships of travel, always his travel, from southern Ohio to coastal New Jersey. Referenced in his letters, in addition to the visits he had made to Belleville in 1844 and 1851 were visits to Eagleswood in the fall of 1854, the summer of 1855, the summer or fall of 1856, October of 1858, the fall of 1859, and another he contemplated making in the spring of 1861. He also saw Sarah in the fall of 1855 at her friend Harriot Hunt's home in Boston.[79] In 1854 Sarah invited Frederick to move to Eagleswood, an invitation over which he "hesitated much" before declining it.[80] But he looked forward to all of his visits, and stayed long enough to keep some of his books with Sarah and the Welds.[81]

An unfortunate misperception of Frederick's character might have been a casualty of time constraints Professor Lerner encountered at the end of a 1996 visit to the Clements Library, as she sought to resolve a question that had arisen, as to which of the sisters was the author of an unsigned manuscript in the Weld-Grimké archive which Lerner subsequently published in her anthology, *The Feminist Thought of Sarah Grimké,* as an essay entitled "Marriage."[82] Lerner's attribution of its authorship to Sarah was contradicted by one of Frederick's letters, commenting approvingly on the work as "Angelina's Article on Marriage." [83] Lerner stated that the letter came to her attention on "the day before I was going to leave [Ann Arbor] for home," when she had thought "all was well" with her identification of Sarah as the essay's author. Lerner resolved the contradiction by hypothesizing that Sarah had been so intimidated by what Lerner supposed was Frederick's disdain for her intellectual capacity, that she "had hesitated to submit her essay on marriage to him under her own name and had conspired with Angelina to pass it off as Angelina's."[84] As Lerner acknowledged, such an explanation required postulating that Angelina joined in the conspiracy by transcribing in her own handwriting the copy Frederick saw. But deception is not characteristic of any of the Grimké siblings in dealings with one another. Here, moreover, evidence refuting Lerner's hypothesis was near at hand. In the next preceding of his letters in the Weld-Grimké archive, one written earlier that year in anticipation of an upcoming visit to Eagleswood, Frederick told Sarah, "I promise myself some pleasure in hearing you read your essay on the U.S., and I should like to hear an essay also from Angelina." Nor does one have to look far in Frederick's correspondence for indications of respect for Sarah's intelligence and compliments for her good judgment. In the same letter he expressed his concurrence with her having deferred action on a matter of family estate business over which they had previously corresponded, so that they could "talk it over" during the upcoming visit, while assuring her that "I highly approve" of other actions she had taken in the matter. And he concluded the letter by continuing a dialog such as he would hardly have had with someone he did not credit for an unusually high degree of intellectual sophistication:

> With regard to your question "Is what Compte says of the sacerdotal order true" the synopsis discloses what he means by the sacerdotal order, and that it is the antipodes of what Guizot would be understood as saying.[85]

In Frederick's next letter, the one in which he identified Angelina as the author of the "Marriage" text, he reaffirmed an instruction concerning his essay, *The Rights of Women in a Democratic Republic,* which he had entrusted to Sarah during the winter of 1856-57, hoping that she could place the work for publication. Here in this November 23, 1858 letter he repeated an earlier request that it be published anonymously: "With regard to my Essay on Woman you recollect that I requested <u>particularly</u> that it be published anonymously, and I have no doubt you will <u>gratify my wish</u> [his underscoring]." But Lerner, misreading "my Essay" as "*your* Essay," and thus supposing it to have been Sarah's work, took Frederick's request for anonymous publication as "a rebuke to Sarah."[86]

Something Sarah did write was the subject of remarks in another of Frederick's letters, which Lerner misinterpreted as "scathing." Sarah had earlier referred to this work in a June 28, 1857 letter to her friend Harriot Hunt, describing it as "a home-spun essay on the query, 'Ought woman to have the election franchise.'" "Well now," she had told Harriot, "I want to find out whether it had better be published, whether it will really serve the cause and then how to get the wherewithal to publish it."[87] Two years later, apparently in a letter to Frederick, Sarah told him what had become of the essay. His response (characteristically lacking question marks) is quoted here exactly as Lerner did:

> I received safely your communication on the right of female suffrage; but why did you select such an inferior journal to publish in. Can it be possible that there is not one in the whole East, which has a commanding character, and extensive influence. I presume, however, that you regard the pages which you have written, [as] merely tentative, as only preparatory to a wider, and more thorough investigation.[88]

The journal in which Sarah published this work on female suffrage must indeed have been "inferior," for, so far as is known, neither that publication nor any other text of the completed work has yet been found by researchers.[89] Here Lerner mistook Frederick's suggestion that Sarah might have intended to set forth only tentative conclusions, to confirm Lerner's hypothesis that Sarah had earlier concealed the authorship of "Marriage" to avoid the humiliation of his supposed disdain for her literary endeavors. Lerner wrote:

> The tone of this letter, as of his other letters, was patronizing in its unquestioned authoritative stance. Sarah had sent him an essay; he dismissed it as merely a tentative draft, without bothering to give any reason for such dismissal. If he had done this

in 1859, he might have done it earlier. If so, was it possible that Sarah had hesitated to submit her essay on marriage to him under her own name and had conspired with Angelina to pass it off as Angelina's?[90]

But Frederick, in his own writing efforts, was well used to trying experiments. "I am very glad you found my letter containing <u>in words</u> a repudiation of the ch [chapter in his treatise] on slavery," he wrote in November, 1858. "Of course you now know that I intended to say no such thing, and it becomes a <u>sacred</u> duty on your part to <u>obliterate</u> it, or <u>burn the letter</u> [his underscoring]."[91] Even when criticizing something Sarah had written, Frederick acknowledged Sarah's capacity for rational thought. "Your observations with regard to the proof of the existence of a God, as deductible from the light of Reason, are not satisfactory," he told her. "I wish you would give your mind to this subject. You may be able to shed some light upon it," for "I have promised myself that you are a thinker."[92]

Enthusiastic for works of European intellectuals, Frederick recommended several to Sarah, all written in French. One (Charles Sismondi's *Histoire des Francais*) consisted of thirty one volumes; others (writings of French mathematician and philosopher Auguste Comte) were of nearly impenetrable intellectual density.[93] Of course it was unrealistic for him to suppose that she could ever have found time to read these works in their entirety. But his recommending them reflected deep respect for Sarah's intellect. The same may be said of a wish – perhaps better described as a dream – for her future, expressed in a letter he wrote in 1860. "Has it occurred to you," he asked, "that there ought to be a professorship of modern, as well as of ancient history? And would it not be well to take that place yourself?"[94]

Fondness in their relationship is evident in the pleasure Sarah took in having Frederick become acquainted with her friend Harriot Hunt. In March, 1853 when she learned that Hunt and a companion were planning a trip to attend a woman's rights convention in Ohio, and supposing that might be an opportunity for meeting Frederick, Sarah wrote describing him as "an old bachelor of the first water, a man of few words . . . retiring to a fault . . . preferring the society of historians & philosophers to the idlers of a ball room" who "loves his sisters and hardly knows anything of any other woman." Sarah provided a letter of introduction when she wrote to Hunt again. In 1855, two years later, Sarah, Hunt, and Frederick were together in Hunt's home in Boston.[95]

Further recounting that last day of her 1999 Clements Library visit when she had been so pressed for time, Professor Lerner wrote:

> I continued reading Frederick Grimké's letters. Many of them were missing, *and only a few of her letters to him are extant* [emphasis supplied]."[96]

How greatly does one wish that the latter were the case. But in fact *there is no letter from Sarah to Frederick* in the Weld-Grimké archive or anywhere else in present existence, so far as is known.

Sarah's Notebooks

The manuscript "notebooks" in which Sarah recorded her thoughts on women's issues after her return to Eagleswood, are folios. In blank they resemble bluebooks in which students wrote examination papers before the advent of portable typewriters and laptops. Cover pages bearing what might be sequential numbers – "No. 2," or "No. 3," but none with "No. 1" – suggest a possibility of earlier such writings, now lost, or perhaps discarded when their content was transcribed into notebooks which survive. Neither their cover pages nor individual entries are dated. Nor is there anything extant from Sarah herself which expresses articulately any intention as to ultimate use of these writings. Passages addressed directly to readers suggest that she envisioned turning them into published works.[97] Surprisingly, in contrast to her 1830's writings, and despite its prominence in contemporary public discourse, the notebooks contain practically nothing about slavery. And notably missing in respect to women's rights are the biblical arguments on which Sarah founded the claims she made in 1838, in her *Letters on the Equality of the Sexes and the Condition of Woman*.

When Elizabeth Ann Bartlett first saw the notebooks in the Weld-Grimké archive she found their content to be "rough, with many additions and deletions, quotations sometimes randomly thrown in, sometimes without clear beginning and concluding paragraphs, often with long run-on sentences or without any sentence structure at all."[98] After considerable editorial subvention by transposing parts of the text into different sequences, inserting paragraph breaks and modern punctuation, and rephrasing some passages, Professor Bartlett published portions in 1988 as essays entitled "The Education of Women," "Condition of Women," "Essay on the Laws Respecting Women," "Marriage," and "Sisters of Charity." Similar revisions of manuscript texts were made by Professor Lerner for excerpts she published in 1998, in *The Feminist Thought of Sarah Grimké*, as "The Education of Women," "Marriage," and "Sisters of Charity." Lerner published the latter two works again in her 2004 "revised and expanded" edition of *The Grimké Sisters of South Carolina.* In none of Bartlett's or Lerner's publications are their modifications specifically noted, or linked by reference to original notebook texts.

Two of the notebooks both have "Education of Woman" on the cover. One of them, considerably shorter in length, has content also found in the other, some of it in passages in which many changes have been made by inserted additions and deletions. It appears, then, that the shorter "Education of Woman" notebook was the earlier in time, and the contents of this, what we will here call the "earlier" notebook, were transposed into the other, here called the "later" notebook, as its first entries. Thus, generally speaking, and bearing in mind that changes to the later notebook's text were probably made at different times, a given passage might have as many as three versions: (1) as it first appears in the earlier notebook; (2) as it next appears initially in the later notebook; and (3) as it finally appears in the later notebook, with all subsequent changes

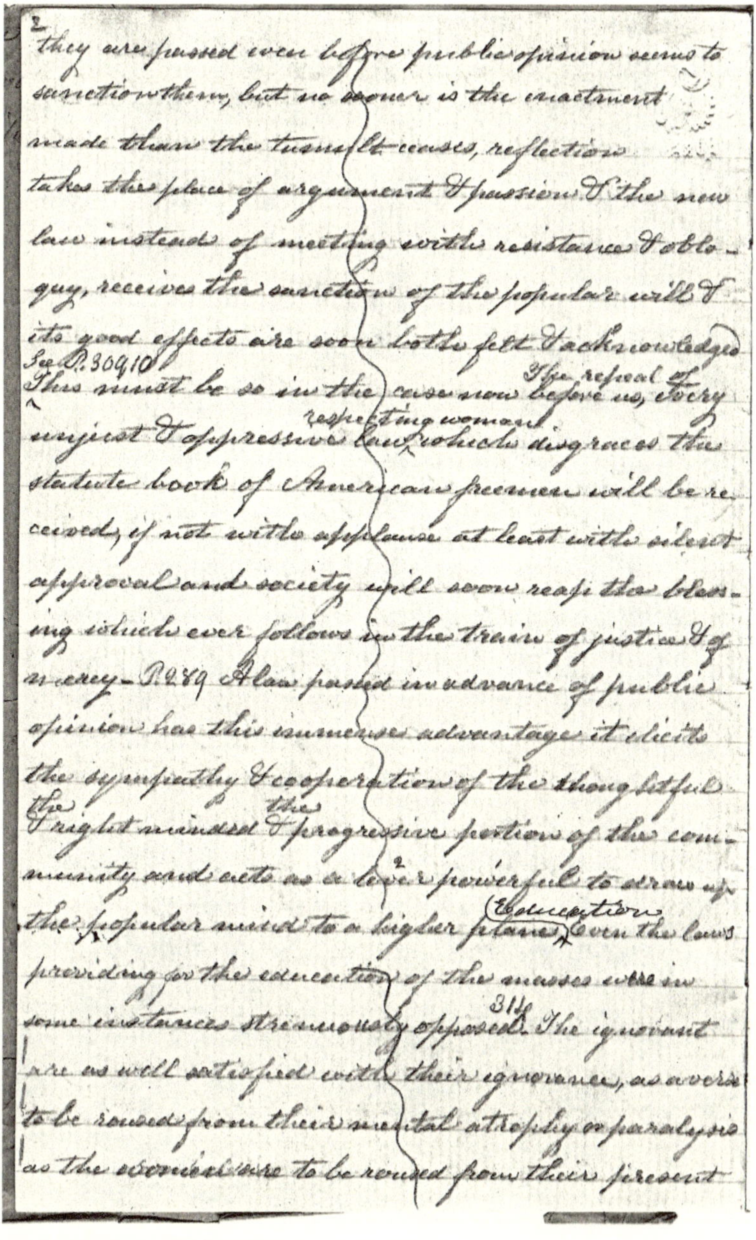

Illustration 6: Sarah Grimké, earlier "Education of Woman No. 2" notebook, p.2. William L. Clements Library, University of Michigan

Curious Numbers, and What They Mean

Illustration 6 is a copy of the earlier "Education of Woman" notebook's second page. Here transcribed to make it easier to follow, the text advances Sarah's contention, citing experience with the "Maine Liquor Law," an early Prohibition statute, that reform measures that initially confront substantial opposition gain increased public acceptance after being enacted into law. (As a convention, quotations of this and other portions of Sarah's notebook texts will here be set forth in italics.) Referring to such laws, Sarah wrote that:

> . . . *they were passed even before public opinion seems to sanction them, but no sooner is the enactment made than the tumult ceases, reflection takes the place of argument and passion and the new law instead of meeting with resistance and obloquy receives the sanction of the popular will and its good effects are soon both felt and acknowledged. See P. 309,10. This must be so in the case now before us. The repeal of every unjust and oppressive law respecting women which disgraces the statute book of American freemen will be received, if not with applause at least with silent approval and society will soon reap the blessing which ever follows in the train of justice and of mercy - P. 289. . . .*

Continuing at the bottom of the same notebook page, after the inserted heading "Education," Sarah wrote:

> *Even the laws providing [for]the education of the masses were in some instances strenuously opposed 312. The ignorant are as well satisfied with their ignorance, as averse to be roused from their mental atrophy or paralysis, as the women are to be roused from their present . . .*

The attentive reader will have spotted arabic numbers appearing in these texts, several prefaced with "P." Such numbers with or without the "P" are found elsewhere in Sarah's notebook manuscripts. But so far as is known they have not previously been noticed, nor their significance understood, by researchers.

The numbers refer to similarly numbered pages of the second, 1856 edition of Frederick's treatise, *The Nature and Tendency of Free Institutions* (hereinafter sometimes referred to as "the treatise," or "treatise," or *"Free Institutions 2d"*). Sarah's "P. 289" notation references this passage, found at treatise-page 289:

> It is sometimes necessary to force a law, in order to bring about a given result . . . . The manifestation of public opinion is not clear and decisive, until they [laws] are actually passed: they show a title to obedience, as well as respect. The desired reform becomes more instead of less popular. It then represents a definite number of people who derive support from a mutual sympathy, and who, through the medium of the same principle of sympathy, gradually impart their opinions to a still wider

number. If any of the American States succeed in
abolishing the traffic in spirituous liquors, it will be
on this principle.

The "P. 309,10" citation above the eighth line of the same page
of Sarah's notebook text refers to a passage on pages 309 and
310 of *Free Institutions 2d*, in which Frederick had contrasted the
initial opposition to laws abolishing religious establishments in
New England, with the wide approval such laws eventually gained,
even by members of formerly favored sects.

Apparently a later insertion, the "312" reference found near
the bottom of the page cites another example from the treatise:
initial public opposition to education reform. In a passage on that
page Frederick had portrayed the clergy as frequent adversaries of
reform measures. Sarah cited this passage again in another "312"
citation of on page 5 of the same (earlier) "Education of Woman"
notebook, for her spirited condemnation of men of the cloth as
"enemies of Truth," who had "done more to sustain war than the
army." Double underscoring for emphasis is rare in Sarah's notebook
writings. Frederick's treatise-page 312 judgment of the clergy was
more temperate: he held their power as allies of government to be
comparable to the military's, but he did not condemn ministers of
religion as warmongers.

The uses Sarah made of *Free Institutions 2d* extended far
beyond harvesting it for illustrations to support her arguments. As
we come to follow others of her treatise-page references, we will
see that she took a major tenet of her brother's political thought, and
by extending its application, used it to inform views of American
women's situation and prospects, which she articulated in the

notebooks. We need first, however, to ground our inquiry in a clearer temporal context, and to develop a better understanding of the work to which the page references in Sarah's notebooks point.

Establishing Sequence and Chronology: Frederick's *Free Institutions 2d*, his *Rights of Women* Essay, and Sarah's Notebooks

Among the valuable insights that discovery of *Free Institutions 2d* page references at the beginning of the earlier of Sarah's "Education of Woman" notebooks provides, is that she wrote those texts after the treatise was in print, and after she had received a copy. Other information makes it possible to establish a rough chronology of those events. Frederick had a Cincinnati friend, William Greene, who proofread *Free Institutions 2d* after it had been set in type by Derby & Jackson, its Cincinnati printer. In a June 14, 1856 letter, Frederick complained to Greene of the Derby firm's failure to furnish bound copies of the work as soon as the pages had been printed. On July 3d he wrote again to Greene, complaining of the inadequacy of Derby's apology for delay in providing such copies.[99] Thus it was sometime in June, 1856, when *Free Institutions 2d* came into physical existence as a book; and whenever it was that Sarah first received a copy would establish a "not before" date for the entries in her "Education of Woman" notebooks, which cite to printed pages of the treatise's text. An April 22, 1857 letter from Frederick enclosing a "list of Errata in Free Institutions which you must correct in your copy," indicates that she had the book at least by then. But there is nothing in the

Weld-Grimké archive to indicate that "your copy" was delivered by mail - no forwarding letter, nor any such letter as Frederick might subsequently have written in response to a comment Sarah might plausibly have included with her (now lost) acknowledgment of receipt. The absence of such correspondence leaves open, although it does not exclude, the possibility of Sarah's having received her copy of the newly published second edition of Frederick's treatise in some way other than by mail delivery.

We know that such was the case as to the manner of Sarah's receiving a manuscript copy of his *Rights of Woman* essay, for in the same April 27, 1857 letter, in which Frederick enclosed the *Free Institutions 2d* errata sheet, he requested that she "make no alterations in the Essay I left with you [underscoring added]." He could only have done that on a visit to Eagleswood, one that must have occurred well before February 1, 1857, when (as recounted above, in the Introduction) Sarah wrote to her friend Harriot Hunt, telling of her considerable efforts to find a publisher for the work.

The pattern established by Frederick's visits to the sisters as they took place, at approximately yearly intervals and never in the winter months, points to a time during the spring, summer or fall of 1856 as the setting for a single visit, the one here in question. But Frederick's preoccupation with getting *Free Institutions 2d* through the printer, until early July, 1856, narrows that time frame to one from mid-summer through the fall of that year. He would undoubtedly have brought a copy of his newly published treatise, along with the manuscript copy of his *Rights of Women* essay. Frederick would have been eager to share both works with Sarah.

Free Institutions: from First to Second Editions

Frederick published two editions of his treatise during his lifetime, in 1848 and 1856. His executor published a third in 1871, posthumously, pursuant to a direction given in Frederick's will. Harvard University Press published a modern edition in 1968 under its Belknap Press imprint, which runs to over six hundred pages not counting a valuable introduction by the edition's editor, the late Professor John William Ward. The work is not an easy read. Maxwell Bloomfield, a scholar who has written of Frederick's legal career, judged it to have "a dry, spare style whose monotonous lucidity was calculated to try the patience of the most sympathetic reader."[100] Well, perhaps it would, if one were to read it straight through from cover to cover. But taking *Free Institutions* in segments, as a series of organized but differently focused disquisitions, would be quite tolerable.

The work has been blighted from the time of Frederick's death by his views on secession and slavery and, in modern times, by his views on race. His contention that each state had a constitutional right to secede from the Union was not without some respectable legal support before the Civil War, and indeed it is hard to imagine that the Constitution could have won approval in the key states of Massachusetts, New York and Virginia, had delegates to their ratification conventions understood that the action they were being called upon to take was irrevocable.[101] Frederick's view of African slavery in the U.S. was moderate for southerners of his time: he deplored the enslavement of African peoples and the circumstances which brought them to the American South, and he disagreed with the U. S. Supreme Court's Dred Scott decision, which

denied inhabitants of territories about to become states the right
to decide for themselves whether slavery should be extended and
established there.[102] But he saw no practical and humane alternative
to maintaining it indefinitely where it existed. His false perception
of Africans' racial characteristics was typical, then, of most whites
in the South and many in the North.[103]

Commentators have differing views of the most significant
of the treatise's teachings. For Professor Ward, writing in his
introduction, "the remarkable thing" was its portrayal of how U.S.
government institutions are kept under constitutional restraint.
Frederick contended that effective limitation of a republican
government's authority is not so much from structural checks and
balances, as from the power that people out of government are
able to exercise over its policies and actions. Ward called this the
"constituent power principle."[104] But a reader who brings to a first
encounter with *Free Institutions* an interest in human rights cannot
fail to be fascinated by a deeper insight.

The words of the treatise's full title, *The Nature and Tendency
of Free Institutions,* are the keys. The seminal element in the *nature*
of American democratic polity, in Frederick's view, is *equality*:
"the only agent which, united with property and education, will
conduce to the right ordering of society."[105] "The wisest plan," he
wrote, is "to communicate equal rights to the people – to throw
them indiscriminately together instead of dividing them into fixed
orders." People are thus "compelled to associate freely, and this
ultimately ripens into a confirmed habit." It is the product of that habit
that excited Frederick. "Free institutions are the only instrument
on a large scale for *elevating the general condition of the people*,"
he wrote, "because they are the only species of government which

is capable of being converted into an instrument of moral and not merely of political discipline for all classes [italics supplied]."[106] Thus the *tendency* of equality, he believed, is to promote not only the betterment of society, but the improvement of its members' individual lives. "The more thoroughly the maxim of equality is taught," he asserted, "the more numerous will be the persons who will strive to make themselves equal to the wisest and best. More vigor, enterprise, and intelligence will be imparted to everyone."[107] Thus in every extension of the right to vote Frederick found a dividend – an improving effect on those newly enfranchised:

> The tendency everywhere at the present day is to extend the [voting] privilege. For every enlargement of it increases the demand, by raising up a greater number of people who are fitted to exercise it. The improvement of the political institutions and the improvement of the population go hand in hand.[108]

He found a comparable dividend for extending access to education. He would "throw knowledge in the way of every one . . . so that men in the pursuit of their daily avocations, and government in the discharge of its official duties, may be compelled to run the same career of improvement." In this way, he believed, "the maintenance of civilization, and the more direct aim which the institutions of government contemplate, are both answered at the same time."[109] For individuals the effect was to impart "vigor and activity to their whole character," thus *giving men new faculties and not merely new rights.*"[110]

So . . . what about extending the franchise, along with improved educational opportunities, to women?

In *Free Institutions'* first edition, published in 1848, Frederick wrote that permitting only males to vote was "a mere abstract limitation," comparable to a minimum voting age. His "equality" argument applied to social class, not to gender:

> It is not the mere abstract limitation of the right which is to be complained of [as too restrictive]. For none but males are now admitted; and as to them, the age of twenty-one is arbitrarily fixed upon as the commencement of the right. It is the restriction of the privilege by a section of the community (as in the European governments) which constitutes the chief ground of objection.[111]

This passage is not monotonous but, as to the logic of women being excluded from voting, it certainly lacks lucidity. Nothing in Frederick's theory of political equality limits his perception of the benefit of extending voting rights, to a good enjoyable only by a society's male members. In 1848, perhaps, like most other American males, he simply took the limitation as a given – a matter unnecessary to mention, or reflect upon. But if that might account for the first edition of his treatise's having nothing to say about women in American political life, then surely one would look for at least something on that subject in the second edition, published in 1856 after momentous developments in the public advocacy of women's rights had occurred. The omission is especially remarkable in view of the closeness of Frederick's contacts with those developments, not only in respect to their proximity, but as objects of his own supportive interest.

The Sisters, Frederick, and the
1850's Feminist Movement

From its organizational inception at a convention in Seneca Falls, New York, in 1848, the American feminist movement made immediate and rapid progress, both in publicizing its objectives and in utilizing political processes for their achievement. The tactics it employed for gaining favorable publicity are still used by political activists: stage a happening that attracts public notice and contrive to influence how the media report it. Thus pioneer women's rights advocates held conventions firmly controlled by organizers who wrote their own reports of the proceedings to encourage favorable, and rebut unfavorable, newspaper coverage. In addition to meetings with local or regional attendance were conventions with delegates from all of the New England, middle-Atlantic, and Midwestern states where the movement had significant support. These "national" conventions came to be identified consecutively, as the "second," "third," and so forth. Organizers would issue a call, hire a hall for a two or three-day session, invite prominent members of the movement or its sympathizers to speak or send letters to be read, and prepare a set of resolutions to be deliberated by a committee and reported favorably to the convention floor for ratification. The proceedings were open to the public. Some were attended by men coming to decry or ridicule, and several ended in disorder. But women's rights conventions were news, and coverage in mass circulation newspapers brought public attention to the movement's demands.

Although both Grimké sisters followed them with interest, Angelina had the greater contact with the conventions, especially during their early years as they acquired a regular format. Whether she personally attended any of these meetings is uncertain.[112] But there is no doubt as to her standing among convention goers and organizers, who recognized Angelina as a leader of the women's rights movement. In 1851 and 1852 she was a member of the "central committee" which provided organizational continuity for the first two or three of the "national" conventions.[113] Her views as to the permanent organization the movement should have were especially influential. Delegates to a convention held in Syracuse in September, 1852 were impressed by a letter she wrote to be read at that meeting, "fearing I might not come."[114] Later published as a tract, it argued against a monolithically structured national body, favoring instead a flexible organization taking its form and selecting its leaders *ad hoc* from meeting to meeting. "Freedom of thought is not nurtured by Organization," Angelina wrote with a capital "O." "Its [a capital-O Organization's] office is to think for the masses, and cast public opinion in its own mold. It builds walls around itself for its own protection." Women "need no external bonds to bind us together," she insisted.[115] Sarah's friend Harriot Hunt, who was present when this letter was read to the delegates, recalled it in her autobiography as "what most attracted my mind at this convention."[116] When Sarah sent Frederick the convention report containing the letter, he read it "with great interest," finding it to be "remarkably well-written, and well-conceived . . . impossible not to appreciate highly." "I have perused and reperused it," he told Sarah. "The stand taken against organization is singularly judicious."[117]

But something else in the convention report brought forth Frederick's ire. Gerrit Smith, a wealthy New Yorker who supported reform causes and frequently appeared at women's rights gatherings, attended this Syracuse convention and was appointed a member of the committee to draft resolutions. One of them proposed that "every woman should engage herself in Literature, the Fine Arts, Professions, Agriculture, [and] Commerce." Smith began a floor speech by observing that "the women who are engaged in this movement are ridiculed as aspiring to be doctors, lawyers, clergymen, sea captains, Generals, Presidents, etc. For the sake of the argument, I admit that this is true, and that they are totally unfit for these places."[118] This unfitness characterization was clearly hypothetical, made as Smith himself stated, "for the sake of argument." But Frederick read it as having been asserted either seriously or provocatively. "Does he really intend what he says, and is the silence of the convention [in other delegates' failure to object] . . . ascribable to the awe in which the convention stood, of a man of his immense wealth?" he wrote in a letter to Sarah. "If this last is the case," Frederick continued (recalling Angelina's admonition to the delegates), "then there is Organization already."[119] Written in April, 1853 while he was working on the second edition of *Free Institutions*, this letter is the first expression in correspondence which survives, of Frederick Grimke's sympathetic interest in the women's rights movement's demands for vocational equality. In his essay, *The Rights of Women in a Democratic Republic*, he would come to cite "the very remarkable conventions which are now frequently held in the United States," describing them as manifesting "an entire alteration in [women's] disposition and character."[120]

Feminist Agitation in Ohio, 1849-1857

In Ohio, as in other states, two constitutional processes were employed to translate feminist demands into political action. Petitioning, recognized as a "right of the people" in state constitutions as well as in the U.S. Constitution's First Amendment, had been employed frequently in the early decades of the republic to communicate citizens' needs or desires for governmental action. Business incorporations, municipal charters, highway improvements, claim payments, and even divorces were among the boons routinely sought from legislatures by petition. For reform causes, organized solicitation of great numbers of petition signatures was an effective pressure tactic, even when the official response was negative or hostile. Thus the infamous "gag rule," adopted at the behest of southern state congressmen to prohibit mere receipt by the U.S. House of Representatives of abolitionists' petitions to eliminate slavery in the District of Columbia, backfired when the rule itself became notorious as an example of slavery's corrosive effect on a right of all citizens.[121]

Another process which served reform causes was one for getting a state constitution amended. That was and still is formidably difficult for amending the U.S. Constitution, given Article V's requirements variously involving actions of Congress and the states by super-majorities (2/3ds for proposing, 3/4ths for ratifying amendments). But for state constitutions, the amendment process was easier. In some states a convention was a permitted – in early Ohio, it was the only – vehicle for adopting constitutional amendments, subject to ratification voted by the electorate. But unlike the body which met in Philadelphia in 1787 to frame the U.S.

Constitution, state constitutional conventions had popularly elected delegates, and their proceedings were conducted in public, reported in the press, and attracted direct citizen input. So it is not surprising that mid-nineteenth century state constitutional conventions in places where feminists were active – New York in 1846, Indiana and Ohio both with sessions in 1850 and 1851, and Massachusetts in 1853 – were all targeted by the women's rights movement.

The first session of Ohio's constitutional convention was shortly preceded by a women's rights convention held in the town of Salem, called by promoters who declared their "feeling that a Convention of men to amend the Constitution of *our* (?) State presents a most favorable opportunity of agitation [original italics and parenthetical question mark]."[122] This "feeling" was strong enough to inspire a campaign of mass petitioning to support the presentation of women's rights demands at the Ohio convention, then only two months from convening. Led by women with political experience in abolitionist and temperance causes, the campaign was impressive even in comparison with present-day mass petitioning efforts. It was cleverly designed to associate a feminist demand that many male Ohioans already favored, with one that most would oppose. Thus a petition for abolishing married women's legal disabilities in respect to contracting capacity, custody of children after divorce, and ownership and control of property – demands the legislature was expected to grant without any express constitutional mandate – had 7,901 signers, while the petition demanding the right to vote had markedly fewer, 2,106 signers.[123] When the latter came to the convention floor in February, 1851 on a motion to strike "male" as a limitation of the state constitution's grant of the franchise,

Illustration 7. "Ohio Women's Rights Convention, held at Akron May 28th and 29th 1851," *New York Picayune*, Jun. 21, 1851

it was overwhelmingly rejected. According to one account the official transcript of the debate had to be sanitized, some delegates' remarks being "dropped from the records, because they were so low and obscene."[124]

But it was not long thereafter when Ohio feminists' demands began to be received courteously and taken seriously. A report of a 1853 women's convention in Cleveland noted "the changed and changing character of the literary and political [news]papers of our State," by several of which "our cause and its advocates have been treated with marked respect, and a disposition has been manifested by many of them to give us direct aid by the circulation of important facts and arguments."[125] In 1857 Caroline Severance was accorded the extraordinary privilege of appearing before the Ohio Senate to read a petition demanding women's suffrage.[126] The response was still "no" – but just barely. A select committee to which the demand was referred reported on it favorably, but a motion in the full Senate to refer it to another committee with instructions to draft a proposed constitutional amendment fell one vote short of passage.

Free Institutions 2d: on Women's Rights - an Awkward Silence

Frederick's sympathetic interest in the women's rights movement as it gathered momentum in the early 1850's, his pride in Angelina's role in determining the movement's organizational structure, and his awareness of the effectiveness by which its goals were being pursued in Ohio through sophisticated political activity, all make it remarkable that the second edition of his treatise, *Free Institutions,* published in 1856, again contains no mention of women's claim to be next in line for admission to full political equality, but simply repeated the first edition's characterization of the franchise's restriction to males as "a mere abstract limitation."[127] The logical, plausible and timely application to American women of the insight Frederick had articulated in the first edition is thus notably missing from *Free Institutions 2d.* We now know that he chose instead to make that application in a separate work, his *Rights of Women* essay, enlisting Sarah as his literary agent to find a publisher.

This choice is not surprising. Demands for women's access to the ballot and entry into occupations outside the home traditionally reserved for males were relentlessly lampooned in the 1850's popular press, whose cartoonists delighted in depicting women wearing the distinctively feminist dress style of short skirt and pantaloons attributed to Amelia Bloomer, publisher of *The Lily*, an organ of the women's rights movement. Although the New York *Tribune* and other leading city newspapers occasionally took serious notice of the cause *The Lily* supported, "Bloomers," were gleefully seized upon by the tabloids as an image for stereotypical portrayals of women's rights advocates, which misrepresented, as their claimed insistence, that women should participate in "men's" occupations not only to the same extent but with complete similarity of workplace lifestyle, social customs, and behavior. The result was a public relations disaster for the movement. The cartoonists, as Kathryn Kohrs Campbell wrote, were "successful in ridiculing the Bloomer costume to death."[128] Gary Bunker put it succinctly in describing the power of their relentless derision: its victims "had two alternatives. They could wait out the storm or protest against the misrepresentation."[129] But Frederick could have done neither.

Citations to *Free Institutions 2d* pages 342 ("immense progress" in "knowledge, industry and the arts" in Europe after 1815) and 351-52 ("military pursuits incompatible with the highest degree of national prosperity") supported Sarah's observation on page 19 of her earlier "Education of Woman" notebook, that "astonishing progress in arts, in science, in literature, in industry" thrives in a climate of international peace, which she believed women's education would foster.[132]

While the earlier notebook's *Free Institutions 2d* page references were not themselves imported with the text Sarah copied into her later "Education of Woman" notebook, she made additional use of the treatise as she added to that text. On page 6 of the later notebook, comparing popular opposition to educational equality for women with resistance to making public elementary school education more widely available, Sarah again cited Frederick's eloquent "The wider the basis . . ." summation by its 28-29 *Free Institutions 2d* page numbers, and this time quoted it directly. On the same notebook page she transcribed another, different passage from treatise page 331, beginning with "General education imparts general freedom of thought . . . ".[133]

Even more numerous are treatise citations in Sarah's "Condition of Woman No. 3," notebook, which addresses suffrage and other political rights she claimed equally for women. Page 2 of this notebook cites a string of *Free Institutions 2d* page numbers – "496 536 544 5 67 573 636" – not proximally connected with any notebook text. These page numbers might have been noted as bookmarks for passages which might be used later in Sarah's writing, as many were. Except for those to treatise-pages 5 (influence of previous

THE ASTOR HOUSE AS IT WILL BE, DURING THE REIGN OF BLOOMERDOM.

*Illustration 8. "*The Astor House as It Will Be During the Reign of Bloomerism*," Yankee Notions,* Nov. 1853.

His contacts with his sisters and the women's rights movement were too close for him to avoid or postpone addressing the topic in some way. But the sophisticated male readership he hoped his *Free Institutions* treatise would impress was not ready for the application of its teachings to American women, and he would have been mortified to see himself as a cartoon character in a publication with an unsophisticated male readership, which might come to the attention of his Chillicothe hotel-boarding tablemates. Frederick was notably sensitive to ridicule even when it was good-natured and, as fellow townsmen observed with amusement, especially when the subject had anything to do with women.[130]

Idea Transfer - from Frederick to Sarah

Sarah took Frederick's perception of the improving effects of allowing disadvantaged groups to gain political rights and educational opportunity, as the basis for her thought about women's place in American society. The evidence for this is pervasive.

A discussion of women's education commencing on page 7 of her earlier "Education of Woman" notebook is preceded by a "28, 9" reference to *Free Institutions 2d,* where, on pages 28 and 29, Sarah found one of the most eloquent affirmations of Frederick's belief that education and enfranchisement operate in parallel, to improve the condition of individual citizens as well as that of society as a whole. He had written:

> The wider the basis on which government is made to stand – that is, the more thoroughly it represents the interests of all orders of men – the firmer the purpose, and the more unremitting the efforts, of individuals in improving their condition. The most effectual way then of raising the intellectual condition of the people is to connect their interests so closely with their improvement, that these may be mutually dependent on each other; to throw knowledge in the way of every one, that it may become of daily use, and indispensable application in both public and private affairs; so that men in the pursuit of their daily avocations, and government in the discharge of its official duties, may be compelled to run the same career of improvement. In this way, the maintenance of civilization, and the more

direct aims which the institutions of government contemplate, are both answered at the same time.

Applying this perception to the situation of American women, Sarah wrote in her notebook:

> *There is nothing more admirably calculated to strengthen a popular government than the unlimited diffusion of education knowledge . . . . The sympathy [and] fellow feeling which universal elementary education produces among a people is even now to be discerned in Am[erica] and its influence in strengthening that sympathy is incalculable when it shall in all its higher branches become the common property of both sexes.*[131]

Agreeing with Frederick that basic education should not be entrusted to religious institutions, she noted on the same notebook page a reference to *Free Institutions 2d* page 330, where he lauded the American system of elementary schools operating under state governmental authority, as one "attended with incalculab[le] advantages to both government and people." And in an uncomple[te] sentence on page 12 of that notebook, where Sarah wrote "[the] great object of popular 331," the page number reference poi[nts to] another statement of Frederick's, to which Sarah, in her t[ime,] would give wider application. In his treatise the statemen[t]

> [T]he great object [of common school education] so to train the youth of the country, that when come to be men, they may render themselves members of society.

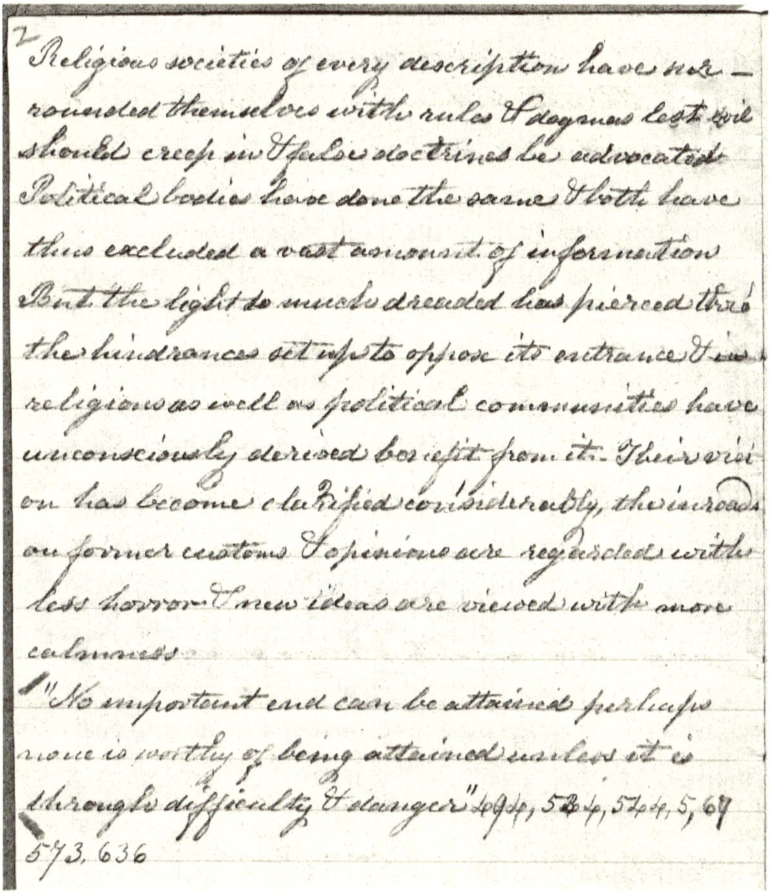
2 Religious societies of every description have sur-
rounded themselves with rules & dogmas lest evil
should creep in & false doctrines be advocated.
Political bodies have done the same & both have
thus excluded a vast amount of information
But the light so much dreaded has pierced thro'
the hindrances set up to oppose its entrance & in
religious as well as political communities have
unconsciously derived benefit from it. Their visi
on has become clarified considerably, their inroads
on former customs & opinions are regarded with
less horror & new ideas are viewed with more
calmness
"No important end can be attained perhaps
none is worthy of being attained unless it is
through difficulty & danger" 494, 534, 544, 5, 67
573, 636

Illustration 9. Sarah Grimké, "Condition of Woman No. 3," notebook, p.2. William L. Clements Library, University of Michigan

civilizations) and 67 (utility of division of labor), all citations in the string and elsewhere in this "Condition of Woman No. 3" notebook connect Sarah's arguments to Frederick's discourse in the concluding section of his treatise, where he addressed expansions of the right to vote as they affected groups marked by differences in social standing, education, and material wealth. On page 496 Frederick had written:

> I know no other plan [than universal suffrage] by which it is possible to keep alive the intelligence of the great bulk of the adult population; none by which it is possible to give activity to the popular mind . . . . [or] by which it is possible to maintain the integrity, industry and activity of public men.

On page 544 he began his chapter on the classes of society with an observation on diversity as a catalyst for social homogenization: "The ultimate effect of a great number of differences [among members of a class] will be to product more uniformity, a greater identity of interests." On page 573 Sarah read his observation that "It is not merely as a political privilege that the electoral franchise is so valuable . . . It causes men to respect and to defer to each other's opinions." And on page 636 she noted his perception that "the enlightened of all countries" had become mutually sympathetic to the betterment of "the community to which [each] belongs," as a distinctive characteristic of the age."

Nowhere in any of her notebooks does Sarah credit her use of *Free Institutions 2d* content to Frederick by name, and she did so only once by description, referring to him as "an able writer." That reference is found on page 11 of her "Condition of Woman No. 3" notebook text where, quoting from treatise page 598, Sarah wrote:

> *May we not compare the condition of woman in every civilized country to that of the younger sons in Italy. There the law of primogeniture prevails,*

and says an able writer: "The younger sons being disinherited, feel little, or no incentive to exertion & live as they can upon the pittance doled out to them by the eldest brother." Hence the number of idle persons is much greater in Italy than in France" where the law of primogeniture is abolished . . . The Italians like the women feel that they are wronged & degraded by the unjust laws which deprive them of property & the natural consequence is inefficiency & unwillingness to exertion. There is no incentive to effort as great as equality. 598.

The passage on treatise page 598 from which Sarah quoted is here set forth in an endnote.[134]

"Why We Desire an Education"
- Sarah's Notebook Texts

Sarah's receipt of *The Rights of Women in a Democratic Republic* was another, at least the third, of her direct encounters with the hypothesis that, when better educated, American women would have productive careers in professional and other higher-end occupational workplaces. We have seen that, by an undisclosed deletion, she suppressed her brother Thomas's rejection of that hypothesis in his essay on women's education, as she quoted it in her *Letters on the Equality of the Sexes and the Condition of Women*, published in 1838.[135] Later, and especially during the first half of the 1850's, Sarah and other feminists confronted the hypothesis in lampoons of their movement's objectives, the object of relentless vilification by caricature in the popular press.

But unlike its negative portrayals as subjects of these first two encounters, Frederick's vision of educated women's future in his *Rights of Women* essay was remarkably positive and encouraging. Sarah was well aware of all three portrayals when she commenced the notebook writings that expounded her own views, in mature life, of women's position and prospects in American society after they were accorded access to higher education. She brought these views into focus by a rhetorical question, first raised in her earlier "Education of Woman" notebook:

> *But, it may be asked, why we desire an extended education, when we already possess the means of education sufficient for all the duties of women's narrow sphere. What is to be the result of a higher education and privileges, when there is no field for the exercise of her powers after she has spent years in preparing for usefulness[?]*[136]

Sarah introduced this question by taking Frederick's *Free Institutions 2d* discussion of a related question: "what will be the effect of placing men on an equality" respecting improved educational opportunities, and broadening not only its application, to *"men and women,"* but its scope, to embrace the *"ultimate result of placing men and women on an equality in education and in the opportunities for acquiring wealth.*[137] So far as is known, this is the first instance in Sarah's writings of her associating women's access to higher education with opportunities for remunerative work outside the home. And it occurs not only after she had received a copy of her brother's essay, but while she herself was actively attempting to have the essay published in a medium of

THE ASTOR HOUSE AS IT WILL BE DURING THE REIGN OF BLOOMERDOM.

Illustration 8. "The Astor House as It Will Be During the Reign of Bloomerism," *Yankee Notions,* Nov. 1853.

His contacts with his sisters and the women's rights movement were too close for him to avoid or postpone addressing the topic in some way. But the sophisticated male readership he hoped his *Free Institutions* treatise would impress was not ready for the application of its teachings to American women, and he would have been mortified to see himself as a cartoon character in a publication with an unsophisticated male readership, which might come to the attention of his Chillicothe hotel-boarding tablemates. Frederick was notably sensitive to ridicule even when it was good-natured and, as fellow townsmen observed with amusement, especially when the subject had anything to do with women.[130]

Idea Transfer - from Frederick to Sarah

Sarah took Frederick's perception of the improving effects
of allowing disadvantaged groups to gain political rights and
educational opportunity, as the basis for her thought about women's
place in American society. The evidence for this is pervasive.

A discussion of women's education commencing on page 7 of
her earlier "Education of Woman" notebook is preceded by a "28,
9" reference to *Free Institutions 2d,* where, on pages 28 and 29,
Sarah found one of the most eloquent affirmations of Frederick's
belief that education and enfranchisement operate in parallel, to
improve the condition of individual citizens as well as that of
society as a whole. He had written:

> The wider the basis on which government is made
> to stand – that is, the more thoroughly it represents
> the interests of all orders of men – the firmer the
> purpose, and the more unremitting the efforts,
> of individuals in improving their condition. The
> most effectual way then of raising the intellectual
> condition of the people is to connect their interests
> so closely with their improvement, that these may
> be mutually dependent on each other; to throw
> knowledge in the way of every one, that it may
> become of daily use, and indispensable application
> in both public and private affairs; so that men in the
> pursuit of their daily avocations, and government in
> the discharge of its official duties, may be compelled
> to run the same career of improvement. In this
> way, the maintenance of civilization, and the more

direct aims which the institutions of government contemplate, are both answered at the same time.

Applying this perception to the situation of American women, Sarah wrote in her notebook:

> *There is nothing more admirably calculated to strengthen a popular government than the unlimited diffusion of education knowledge . . . . The sympathy [and] fellow feeling which universal elementary education produces among a people is even now to be discerned in Am[erica] and its influence in strengthening that sympathy is incalculable when it shall in all its higher branches become the common property of both sexes.*[131]

Agreeing with Frederick that basic education should not be entrusted to religious institutions, she noted on the same notebook page a reference to *Free Institutions 2d* page 330, where he lauded the American system of elementary schools operating under state governmental authority, as one "attended with incalculable advantages to both government and people." And in an uncompleted sentence on page 12 of that notebook, where Sarah wrote "The great object of popular 331," the page number reference points to another statement of Frederick's, to which Sarah, in her thought, would give wider application. In his treatise the statement read:

> [T]he great object [of common school education] is so to train the youth of the country, that when they come to be men, they may render themselves useful members of society.

Citations to *Free Institutions 2d* pages 342 ("immense progress" in "knowledge, industry and the arts" in Europe after 1815) and 351-52 ("military pursuits incompatible with the highest degree of national prosperity") supported Sarah's observation on page 19 of her earlier "Education of Woman" notebook, that "astonishing progress in arts, in science, in literature, in industry" thrives in a climate of international peace, which she believed women's education would foster.[132]

While the earlier notebook's *Free Institutions 2d* page references were not themselves imported with the text Sarah copied into her later "Education of Woman" notebook, she made additional use of the treatise as she added to that text. On page 6 of the later notebook, comparing popular opposition to educational equality for women with resistance to making public elementary school education more widely available, Sarah again cited Frederick's eloquent "The wider the basis . . ." summation by its 28-29 *Free Institutions 2d* page numbers, and this time quoted it directly. On the same notebook page she transcribed another, different passage from treatise page 331, beginning with "General education imparts general freedom of thought . . . ".[133]

Even more numerous are treatise citations in Sarah's "Condition of Woman No. 3," notebook, which addresses suffrage and other political rights she claimed equally for women. Page 2 of this notebook cites a string of *Free Institutions 2d* page numbers – "496 536 544 5 67 573 636" – not proximally connected with any notebook text. These page numbers might have been noted as bookmarks for passages which might be used later in Sarah's writing, as many were. Except for those to treatise-pages 5 (influence of previous

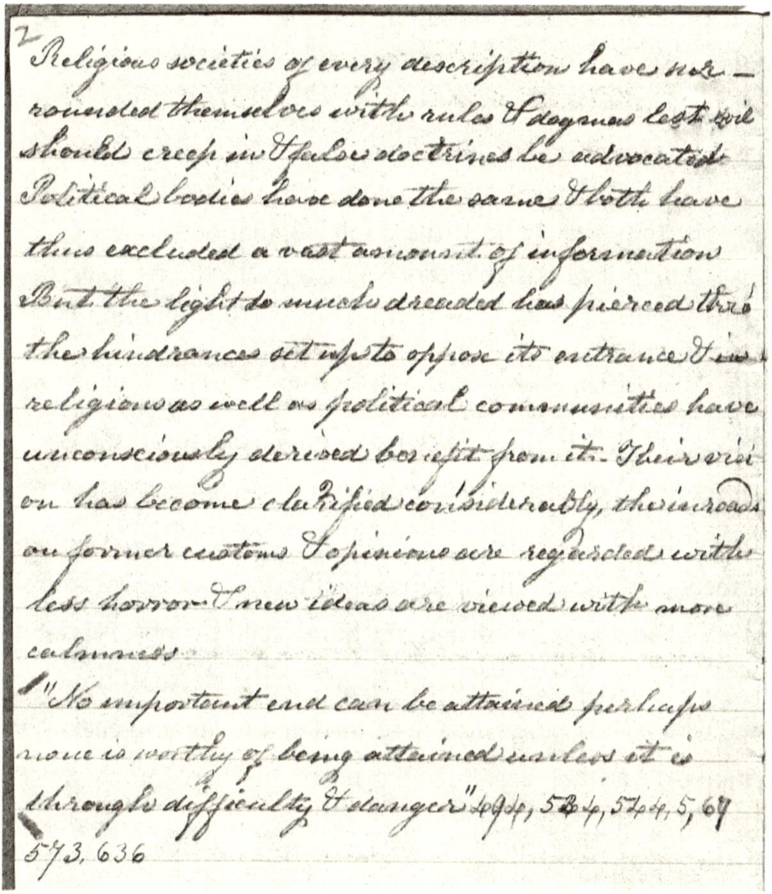

Illustration 9. Sarah Grimké, "Condition of Woman No. 3," notebook, p.2. William L. Clements Library, University of Michigan

civilizations) and 67 (utility of division of labor), all citations in the string and elsewhere in this "Condition of Woman No. 3" notebook connect Sarah's arguments to Frederick's discourse in the concluding section of his treatise, where he addressed expansions of the right to vote as they affected groups marked by differences in social standing, education, and material wealth. On page 496 Frederick had written:

> I know no other plan [than universal suffrage] by which it is possible to keep alive the intelligence of the great bulk of the adult population; none by which it is possible to give activity to the popular mind . . . . [or] by which it is possible to maintain the integrity, industry and activity of public men.

On page 544 he began his chapter on the classes of society with an observation on diversity as a catalyst for social homogenization: "The ultimate effect of a great number of differences [among members of a class] will be to product more uniformity, a greater identity of interests." On page 573 Sarah read his observation that "It is not merely as a political privilege that the electoral franchise is so valuable . . . It causes men to respect and to defer to each other's opinions." And on page 636 she noted his perception that "the enlightened of all countries" had become mutually sympathetic to the betterment of "the community to which [each] belongs," as a distinctive characteristic of the age."

Nowhere in any of her notebooks does Sarah credit her use of *Free Institutions 2d* content to Frederick by name, and she did so only once by description, referring to him as "an able writer." That reference is found on page 11 of her "Condition of Woman No. 3" notebook text where, quoting from treatise page 598, Sarah wrote:

> *May we not compare the condition of woman in every civilized country to that of the younger sons in Italy. There the law of primogeniture prevails,*

and says an able writer: "The younger sons being disinherited, feel little, or no incentive to exertion & live as they can upon the pittance doled out to them by the eldest brother." Hence the number of idle persons is much greater in Italy than in France" where the law of primogeniture is abolished . . . The Italians like the women feel that they are wronged & degraded by the unjust laws which deprive them of property & the natural consequence is inefficiency & unwillingness to exertion. There is no incentive to effort as great as equality. 598.

The passage on treatise page 598 from which Sarah quoted is here set forth in an endnote.[134]

"Why We Desire an Education"
- Sarah's Notebook Texts

Sarah's receipt of *The Rights of Women in a Democratic Republic* was another, at least the third, of her direct encounters with the hypothesis that, when better educated, American women would have productive careers in professional and other higher-end occupational workplaces. We have seen that, by an undisclosed deletion, she suppressed her brother Thomas's rejection of that hypothesis in his essay on women's education, as she quoted it in her *Letters on the Equality of the Sexes and the Condition of Women*, published in 1838.[135] Later, and especially during the first half of the 1850's, Sarah and other feminists confronted the hypothesis in lampoons of their movement's objectives, the object of relentless vilification by caricature in the popular press.

But unlike its negative portrayals as subjects of these first two encounters, Frederick's vision of educated women's future in his *Rights of Women* essay was remarkably positive and encouraging. Sarah was well aware of all three portrayals when she commenced the notebook writings that expounded her own views, in mature life, of women's position and prospects in American society after they were accorded access to higher education. She brought these views into focus by a rhetorical question, first raised in her earlier "Education of Woman" notebook:

> *But, it may be asked, why we desire an extended education, when we already possess the means of education sufficient for all the duties of women's narrow sphere. What is to be the result of a higher education and privileges, when there is no field for the exercise of her powers after she has spent years in preparing for usefulness[?]*[136]

Sarah introduced this question by taking Frederick's *Free Institutions 2d* discussion of a related question: "what will be the effect of placing men on an equality" respecting improved educational opportunities, and broadening not only its application, to *"men and women,"* but its scope, to embrace the *"ultimate result of placing men and women on an equality in education and in the opportunities for acquiring wealth.*[137] So far as is known, this is the first instance in Sarah's writings of her associating women's access to higher education with opportunities for remunerative work outside the home. And it occurs not only after she had received a copy of her brother's essay, but while she herself was actively attempting to have the essay published in a medium of mass circulation. So one would expect that when she proceeded in her notebooks to answer the question she had asked herself: *"What is to be the result of a higher education"* for women, when at present *"there is no field for exercise"* of capabilities thus to be gained – she would respond with a powerful affirmation of Frederick's *Rights of Women* prophesy.

Surprisingly, this was not the case. Beginning on page 14 of her earlier "Education of Woman" notebook, Sarah answered her question as follows:

> *1ˢᵗ then we ask education as a means to an end, that end is greater fitness to fulfil the duties of wife & mother & all the domestic & social relations there can be no attainment too high no learning too profound not to be advantageously turned to account in the sacred circle of <u>Home</u>.*

> *2d We ask it because we covet an enlarged sphere of usefulness; we feel a thirst for knowledge which can only be quenched by drinking freely of the crystal stream of wisdom which flows from under the throne of God.*

> *3d We ask it because we feel as if the time has come when our Father in heaven having awakened new desires, stirred within us new aspirations, was calling upon us to aid with all our powers in promoting the progress of the race.*

She next cited personal sacrifices women often made in order to provide sons or brothers with an education. Then she added a "guarantee":

> *We speak not boastingly we simply state facts*
> *because we believe it will be seen that there is a*
> *guarantee in the love nature of woman that she*
> *never will forsake those duties & enjoyments in*
> *which are centered her highest happiness.*

As she subsequently transcribed this answer to the later "Education of Woman" notebook Sarah made two changes which might be taken as substantive. She left "Home" without any underscoring in her first enumerated response. And she modified the "guarantee" by adding words here set off in bold type:

> *We speak not boastingly, we simply state facts.*
> ***We ask an education because we believe that it***
> ***will exalt & purify woman and will enlarge her***
> ***boundaries of knowledge*** *and because we know*
> *that there is a guarantee in the love nature of woman*
> *that she will never forsake the duties & enjoyments*
> *in which are centered her supreme felicity.*[138]

The double-underscoring of "Home" in the earlier notebook text is another rare instance of Sarah's use of that means of emphasis. If it there stood for emphatic rejection of Frederick's vision of educated women's future, its omission from the later notebook was a more temperate expression of that response. The purport of the second change is clearer: by adding "exalt & purify" to the "guarantee," Sarah reaffirmed the spiritual tenor of her second and third responses, which, as we have seen, already described women's gaining an education as "drinking freely of the crystal stream of wisdom which flows from under the throne of God" and credited "our Father in heaven" for awakening women's desires and aspirations "to aid with all our powers in promoting the progress of the race."

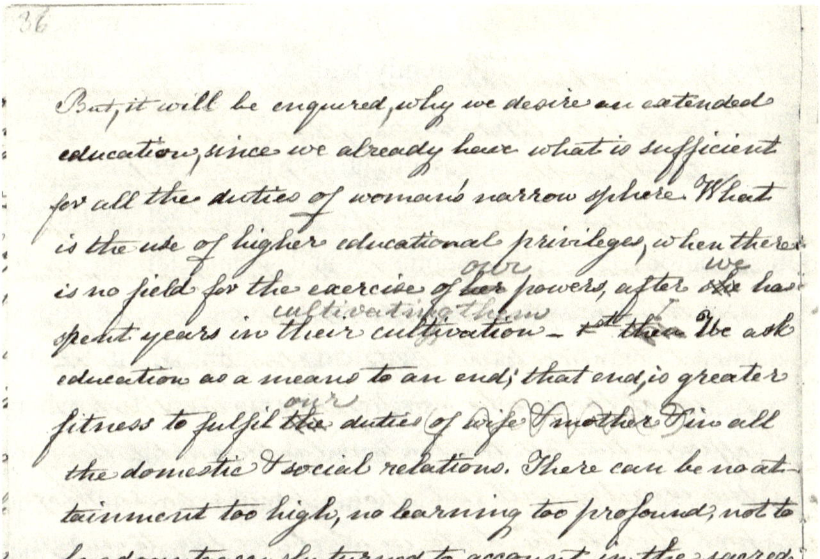

36

But, it will be enquired, why we desire an extended education, since we already have what is sufficient for all the duties of woman's narrow sphere. What is the use of higher educational privileges, when there is no field for the exercise of our powers, after we have spent years in cultivating them – 1st then We ask education as a means to an end; that end, is greater fitness to fulfil our duties of wife & mother & in all the domestic & social relations. There can be no attainment too high, no learning too profound, not to be advantageously turned to account in the sacred circle of Home – 2d We ask it, because we covet an enlarged sphere of usefulness; we feel a thirst for improvement, which can only be quenched by drinking freely of the streams of knowledge – 3d We ask it, because we feel as if the time had come, when God having awakened new desires, and stirred within us new aspirations, was calling upon us to aid with all our powers, in promoting the progress of the race. To God, to the cause of Humanity, we desire to consecrate ourselves, and we ask your aid – Will you

Illustration 10. Sarah Grimké, later "Education of Woman No. 2," notebook, p. 36. William L. Clements Library, University of Michigan

Subsequent modifications of the later notebook's text, written in pencil, might not actually have been made by Sarah. On at least one of several visits to the Weld household a clergyman friend, Rev. E. J. Cutler, was shown the notebooks and invited to suggest textual changes, apparently with a view to publication.[139] That he signed one of the suggestions written in pencil suggests that other penciled-in changes might also have been his.[140] One of those changes replaced "duties of wife and mother" with "our duties," but it left "in all the domestic and social relations" in the first enumerated answer. Another penciled change was substantive: it deleted "opportunities for acquiring wealth" from Sarah's introduction of the *"why we desire an education"* question, where she had cited such opportunities as an element of the status of equality which women aspired to gain. Even if it was Cutler who wielded the pencil, one wonders whether he would have made that change, or how it could have been left to stand, without Sarah's concurrence.

Professor Nancy Cott has found, as a nineteenth century "paradox in the 'progress' of women's history in the United States," that as American men moved from self employment (as farmers, for example, or small business proprietors) to become participants in corporate enterprises with business operations extending far beyond individual employees' home communities, American women remained strongly identified with a "sphere" of domestic life, even as they became better educated, more widely read, and more socially and politically conscious. This "sphere" was the essential feature of what Professor Cott calls the "canon of domesticity." She described it with a collage of quotations taken from contemporary writings, many by women:

[T]he home contrasted to the restless and competitive world because its "presiding spirit" was woman, who was "removed from the arena of pecuniary excitement and ambitious competition." Woman inhabited the "shady green lanes of domestic life," where she found "pure enjoyment and hallowed sympathies" in her "peaceful offices." If man was the "fiercest warrior, or the most unrelenting votary of stern ambition," and "toil worn" by "troubled scenes of life," woman would "scatter roses among the thorns of his appointed track." In the "chaste, disinterested circle of the fireside" only – that is, only in the hearts and minds of sisters, wives and mothers – could men find "reciprocated humanity ... unmixed with hate or the cunning of deceit." The spirit of business and public life thus appeared to diverge from that of the home chiefly because the two spheres were the separate domains of the two sexes.[141]

With all of its modifications, including a few which softened or generalized her expressions (omitting double underscoring of "Home," for example, or substituting "our duties" for "duties of wife and mother"), Sarah's "Education –of –Woman"-notebook answers to "why we desire an extended education" placed the object of that desire – "to fulfil our duties in all the domestic and social relations," by turning such education "to account in the sacred circle of Home" – entirely within the "sphere" of the "canon of domesticity."

Well – almost entirely. An exception hinted at in the second and third answers citing "an enlarged sphere of usefulness" and a divine calling "to aid with all out powers, in promoting the progress of the race," suggests that educated women might do sophisticated work *pro bono* in the world outside the home. In a passage addressed directly to readers found on page 15 of her later "Education of Woman" notebook, Sarah recounted her bitter disappointment in being denied, as a girl, "permission to go hand in hand with my brothers through their studies." On an attached, separate slip of paper she stated that had she "received the education I coveted, and been bred directly to the profession of the law," she might have become "a useful member of society . . . a protector of the helpless and unfortunate, a pleader for the poor and dumb." But she did not aspire to practice as most male lawyers did, to protect clients' interests in private wealth and earn a living for themselves. As she stated in a letter quoted by her friend and first biographer, Catherine Birney, "Women must come into the arena with men, not to increase the number of potsherds, but to elevate the standard of right."[142] It was only for altruistic purposes that Sarah envisioned for educated American women "an enlarged sphere of usefulness" in workplaces outside the home.

That vision is also reflected in another of Sarah's notebooks, one of two with "Condition of Woman" on the cover, which is the manuscript source of the essay Professors Lerner and Bartlett each published as "Sisters of Charity." Sarah took the title from a work by Anna Jameson, a British feminist who recounted women's increasing involvement in efforts to improve conditions in prisons, mental institutions, and hospitals.[143] In her essay Sarah protested women's having been "shut out" by prejudice, from "taking their places wherever intellect rather than strength is required." But the "places" she chose to mention were all for endeavors in the service of social or political reform causes. Her only reference to remunerative occupations was in noting women's losses to machines in factories, of hand-sewing piecework they formerly did at home. Acknowledging the "present misery" of that development in "depriving thousands, if not millions of their daily bread," Sarah nonetheless lauded it as a "grand work," since it compelled women to turn to "other occupations."[144] But she did not connect their entry into any such occupations with higher education.

Sarah's Feminist Theology

Sarah Grimké was intensely spiritual. "Expecting to sail this morning for Philadelphia I desire once more to dedicate myself to the service of God," she wrote in her diary on leaving Charleston in 1821, never to return. That dedication remained steadfast, surviving instability of church affiliations as she converted from Anglicanism to Presbyterianism in Charleston, joined the Quakers a year after coming to Philadelphia and left them in 1836, after Thomas's death, "feeling that I was required to do it and that my Peace depended upon it."[145] From the beginning of her public career as an abolitionist and feminist, and thereafter for the remainder of her life, Sarah belonged to no established church. This disconnect was typical of her generation of feminists, and paradoxical. On the one hand, as Anna Speicher found, "these women, for the most part, distanced themselves from recognized religious groups and movements, and drew their beliefs from a variety of sources." On the other hand, as Professor Cott observed, Protestant faith was "an important generator and legitimator" of nineteenth century feminists' demands. Blanche Hersh summed it up: "reform became the main religion for most of them."[146]

By the mid-1850's Sarah had developed a feminist theology with a clear vision of women's place in God's kingdom on earth, after they gained what she regarded as equality with men and their minds were improved by education. That place was distinctive to their gender, as was Sarah's conception of an equality based on freedom to exploit inherent gender differences. It was women's superior ability to exercise moral and spiritual leadership that would rescue men from lives of brutish subjugation in a "reign of animal power," to find the "radiant advent . . . of the day foreshadowed by Christ, when the feminine spirit, the spirit of love and of holiness, shall be embodied in the character of woman, and *through her* the brotherhood, I would say the sisterhood, of the race be acknowledged and lived [italics added]." Sarah thus described her vision in a May 21, 1856 letter to Jeanne Deroin, a French socialist and feminist, published the following August in *The Lily*, an American women's rights journal.[147]

Implications of that vision for the vocational future of educated American women as Sarah conceived it, were previously revealed in a May 23, 1855 letter to Sarah's friend Harriot Hunt, lauding Hunt's career as a physician. In 1847 Harvard Medical School had denied her application for admission, and when it granted a second application three years later, faculty and student hostility kept her from attending. However, she established a medical practice in Boston and regularly treated female patients. "What an unspeakable blessing it will be to the world," Sarah wrote, if "women of the right stamp" were to become doctors. "No woman can justly fulfill her mission as a physician without a love spirit," and "no woman deserves the name of physician who cannot hold intercourse with the spirits of her patients and minister to their higher nature." Thus, Sarah concluded, "I fear nothing more than that women unblest with this gift and whose highest attainment is the scientific knowledge of medicine should crowd into the profession." Here too, as she indicated in recounting her own dream of becoming a lawyer, a profession to which women could gain access by higher education was to be practiced primarily for altrusitic, not monetary reward. Sarah did not appear ready to accept either Frederick's elegantly phrased prediction in *Rights of Women*, that American women would eventually be "introduced into the engrossing occupations of life," or the plainspoken aspiration of "Mrs. Sockdollager," (a character in a parody of women's rights demands published in *Yankee Notions,* a popular illustrated monthly) to become "a millingitary ossifer, speechify, throw myself onto my country, make money, lose money, and be somebody!"[148]

Sarah's vision of educated women's vocational future was restated a few months later, in an August 4, 1856 letter to Gerrit Smith, which *The Lily* published the following October. Smith was an abolitionist, political activist, social reformer, supporter of women's rights causes, and cousin of another prominent American feminist, Elizabeth Cady Stanton. The letter's full text is here set forth in Appendix C.

Its writing was prompted by Smith's weighing in on the brouhaha over "Bloomers," to which Sarah first responded, saying that while that dress was suited for domestic outdoor activities like working in the garden or "jumping fences," she preferred ordinary "womanly dress" for wear outside the home. She went on to "rejoice that women are gradually introducing themselves into employments from which they have hitherto been excluded," citing the phenomenon as one which "cannot but produce a wider scope for thought, a greater opportunity for intellectual activity, a larger circumference of action," and so "enable woman to take more comprehensive views of herself, her relations to the whole human family, and the co-relation of one thing to another." But the employment opportunities Sarah mentioned in this connection – "clerk, salesman, bookkeeper, &c." – exemplified the "other occupations" cited in her essay "Sisters of Charity" as welcome replacements for jobs women factory workers were losing to machines. None required higher education.

It was "the next generation," as Sarah went on to predict, that would "produce women of higher organization, of finer intellectual and moral development." "Man" too, she thought, would have a significant role in this. Having long regarded woman as his "slave . . . created mainly to minister to his material comfort, to surrender herself to the gratification of his passion and appetites," he had finally begun "to perceive that he possesses a spiritual nature of which he had hardly been cognizant, which demands nutriment of another kind, enjoyments of a higher order." While men had been "pursuing animal gratifications and reveling in the fields of literature and science, woman's love nature had been unfolding and strengthening." It will be recalled that Sarah had referred opaquely to this "love nature" in her notebook answer to "why we desire an education."[149] Here in her letter to Gerrit Smith she described it, declaring that "in her social and domestic relations she [woman] exhibits more tenderness, more patient watchfulness, more power of endurance" – all qualities reflecting "a higher spirituality, a greater devotion to God, a more intimate acquaintance with Christ, a stronger love for the truths of religion, a closer adherence to its precepts than has marked his [man's] character." Accordingly, as man now "begins to look to woman as the channel through which his higher, his spiritual self may receive the nourishment he craves," he will come to feel "that there is something above power and science necessary to satisfy the yearnings of his immortal soul, and that woman is the medium through which he may receive it." But American women had not yet become that medium. "Let us accept her for what she is," Sarah pleaded, "until she learns by experience what kind of woman the age calls for, and bends her powers to become what is needed."

And what, as Smith might have wondered, what would that experience be? "She [woman] is now receiving an education," Sarah wrote, "passing through a discipline which she needs . . . acquiring knowledge which will make her see the necessity of thinking and acting for herself." And then:

> *The time . . . is not far distant when it will be regarded as humiliating to be dependent on a father, husband, brother, cousin, &c, unless circumstances absolutely disqualify a woman for earning her own living . . . .*
>
> *I cannot but hope that this appeal to the heart of woman will operate to rouse her to a sense of her obligations to do what she can towards supplying her own material wants . . . When she encounters the path of usefulness and duty, she cannot but see the incompatibility of her present dress with true womanly dignity. I look forward to the time when her gewgaws and fashions will drop off . . .*

This is a singular instance of Sarah's positing "earning her own living" in occupations for which higher education is requisite, as an aspiration of American women.[150] But she was careful to disclaim any suggestion that the aspiration would be realized at the expense of qualities distinctive to their gender. "It seems to me that we disparage God's work by supposing that he has created two beings essentially the same," she told Smith. "But while I accord to man superiority in physical strength, [and] in all the more hardy and severe departments of the understanding, I must believe that the spiritual nature has been more highly developed in woman than in man, because it is universally conceded that the strength of the moral world lies in woman – that in her heart religion has found its home – that she is from her very organization more susceptible to spiritual impressions." Concluding, Sarah wrote:

> *When these glorious attributes of Deity are embodied in woman's life so far as the finite can approach the Infinite, she will shed around her a rich aroma which will permeate the moral atmosphere as the fragrance of flowers does the natural. But it holds true in this, as in everything relating to the sexes, "Neither is the man without the woman, neither the woman without the man." The present conflict manifests the tendency of humanity towards a new social system – indefinite enough, but radically different from the old. This may be the negative era of social progress, but it is indispensable as a preparation for the advent of that change which will result in the elevation of woman, and the spiritual advancement of man.[151]*

Pressed to Reveal What She Thought of
Rights of Women, What Did Sarah Say?

On March 13, 1858 Frederick wrote to Sarah confiding that he had "probably erred in supposing that the professions, and the employments of civil life, were within the appropriate domain of women" and requesting that she "keep my dissertation, but do not lend it any more." By then it had been eight months since Sarah had reported in a letter to Harriott Hunt that "brother's Essay is still on hand; I cannot tell what is best about it as I cannot get it into any popular periodical." When Frederick next wrote to her in October, 1858, his lack of confidence in the work's conclusions had grown to the point of requesting that it be published, if at all, anonymously. He repeated that request on November 28, 1858, in the letter which would give Professor Lerner difficulty with its identification of Angelina as the "Marriage" essay's author. The letter's mention of October 31ˢᵗ as the date of Frederick's leaving "Orange" [Orange, New Jersey, a stop on the New York and Erie Railroad] on his journey back to Chillicothe suggests that his visit with the sisters ran almost until the end of the month.

An atmosphere of mutual discouragement must have oppressed that visit. Sarah had suffered a humiliating failure to place a controversial work of her own before the public when, in May of that year, she made her only appearance before a women's rights convention. But its New York City venue was notorious for attracting raucous crowds of unsympathetic male attendees, and their rhythmic clapping on this occasion made a pathetic spectacle of Sarah's weakly voiced attempt to speak. "Miss Grimke," according to a derisive *New York Times* account, "read an essay to the convention which no one could hear."[152] Even a sympathetic observer wrote of her performance:

> Why it was dreadful – sheet after sheet, closely written and monotonously read . . . . So low and monotonous her tones that she could not be heard 10 feet from the platform – at last – the audience gave way and there came that dreadful measured thump thump of mock applause which she took all for genuine and looked pleased and said "I can raise my voice if I am not heard" and then they applauded more and more . . . . She has lived out of the world so long that she has forgotten what the world can bear."[153]

Y⁹ MAY SESSION OF Y⁹ WOMAN'S RIGHTS CONVENTION—Y⁹ ORATOR OF Y⁹ DAY DENOUNCING Y⁹ LORDS OF CREATION.

Illustration 11. "Ye May Session of Ye Women's Rights Convention," Vanity Fair, May, 1859

The experience could not have left Sarah eager to encourage a brother abnormally sensitive to criticism and averse to confrontation, to expose himself to the ridicule he would have received had *Rights of Women* appeared in a widely read print medium.

In the same November 28, 1858 letter in which Frederick repeated his request that the essay be published anonymously, he cited his practice of sometimes writing experimentally on both sides of a position he had taken, and asked Sarah to burn something he had recently sent her with arguments to the contrary of his position on slavery. Eight months later, in a letter written July 30, 1859, he mentioned the practice again as one he supposed Sarah herself followed. Apparently referring to her notebook writings, he told her that he presumed that she regarded "the essays which you have written, as merely tentative." Now, he said, he had come to view his *Rights of Women* essay in the same way.

"It is obvious," he went on to write in that July 30, 1859 letter, "that the changes contemplated in the condition of women involve one of the greatest, if not the greatest, revolution which has ever taken place in human affairs," and that they demanded "the same earnest and concentrated mental exertion, as if we were for the first time attempting to unfold any one of the departments of Science." He made this observation, he said, "on my own behalf as well as on yours." Then he defined the problem he believed his essay presented. Sarah was aware, he wrote, "of the doubts which I have entertained, of the entire solidity of the views in my disquisition" despite his having "already in that composition answered nearly all objections." So "to assist me in getting rid of those doubts" he proposed "to engage you in a correspondence on that subject, and

to direct your attention particularly to the following difficulties."
The text here retains his underscoring:

> lst. The distinction universally prevailing in the
> position of the two sexes. In all times and in all
> countries, the destination of the two has been
> widely different. Nor does it appear to be possible
> to assign any reason for this difference, other than
> that it is to be found in an originally different
> constitution of the two. If this be so, then this
> different destination of the two must be natural, that
> is, must be in conformity with laws which control
> society, and which therefore society cannot control.
> The difference is not peculiar to the human race;
> it runs without exception through the whole scale
> of the animal creation. This view suggested by the
> universality of the law, and which I referred to in my
> composition ten years ago, is entitled to profound
> and redoubled attention.
>
> 2d. If this view supposes that this great difference
> has its foundation in an originally different physical
> structure, and conformation, this need not excite
> surprise, for we are to a wonderful extent ruled by
> our physical organization . . . . Even the brain is a
> natural workmanship, the same spirit animates all
> human beings, but the brain which is only the organ
> of the mind, is differently organized in each, and
> creates infinite varieties among individuals. The
> great difficulty in all investigations of moment is
> to generalize our ideas. As soon as we can form
> a happy generalization, we obtain a clue to the
> difficulty.[154]

In a third enumerated point the letter went on to portray "the indiscriminate association of the two sexes" as "fraught with exceeding difficulty," an anticipated result of realizing his vision of educated women's vocational future. But it was the search for a "happy generalization" of men's and women's capabilities and roles that would present the supremely difficult challenge.

The only surviving indication of Sarah's response comes several months later, and it is marked by a puzzling instance of cross-communication. Near the end of the year 1859, on the day of Frederick's arrival for another visit to Eagleswood, Sarah wrote and mailed a letter addressed to him in Chillicothe. He did not see this letter until his return there, when on December 14, 1859 he replied to it as "the letter you mailed to me on the day of my arrival at Eagleswood."[155] Like all of the rest of Sarah's letters to him, this letter is now lost. That it contained her response to Frederick's earlier plea to "assist me in getting rid of [my] doubts" about *Rights of Women* is evident from the tenor of his December 14, 1859 reply:

> The letter which you mailed to me on the day of my arrival at Eagleswood was received safely. The view which you take must certainly be the correct one; that the destination of men and women is different, but it is sometimes very difficult to give a perfectly logical consistency to our ideas, especially on a subject which has been hitherto so carelessly investigated, and it appears to me, that the exceptions which you make, contribute to mar the whole scheme of thought.

Frederick did not describe those "exceptions." Continuing as he tried to define the contradiction they implied, he wrote:

> For the different spheres to which the two sexes are destined, must depend either upon a difference in some of their faculties, or upon the different duties which they are necessarily and naturally called upon to perform, or upon both. Now these seem unequivocally to point to domestic life as the sphere of woman, and the active duties of outdoor life, as that of men. I am by no means satisfied that the intellectual powers of women are inferior to those of men; but you have justly remarked, that men have more physical strength, and activity. But this is in consequence of their having a more robust organization, and the more robust the organization, the more energetic is the will, and even admitting that the intellectual faculties in both are the same, yet this difference in the energy of the will in the two sexes will make a great difference in the exercise and use of those faculties. The economy of nature appears here to be very fine.

Sarah would not have conceded Frederick's facile portrayal of "more robust organization," and greater "energy of the will" as a succession of inevitable consequences of man's superior physical strength. Nor would they have agreed on what he had in mind as he went on to say: "No intellectual faculties are so high, but what they may adorn the sphere of domestic life, the natural and inevitable destination of women . . ." It was not for pleasing "adornment" of married life that Sarah sought equal educational opportunities for women; to the contrary, such opportunities were to qualify them for new and vital roles as their husbands' spiritual mentors, giving marriage a sacred character and purpose.

But it is unlikely that Sarah ever shared that vision with Frederick. For all of the intimacy with which it was surrounded, their intellectual discourse had sharp restrictions as to content. As to slavery, the restriction was one Frederick imposed. Although he was interested in what Sarah thought about some of his opinions on the subject, he had no patience for her opposing views. "I feel very much concerned to think that my [*Free Institutions 2d*] chapter on slavery has given you so much trouble," he wrote on June 10, 1857. "You adopted the same sentiment when on reading it in the first edition, you remarked, 'I differ with you, but I admire a mind that is true to its own convictions.'" But he complained when she communicated her own abolitionist convictions: "You have not written me a single letter during the last twelve months which has not contained something on the subject," he wrote peevishly. "In all frankness," he continued," I really do not wish to read the observations made by the person you allude to." Yet his dismissals were not always so rude. Once when he once summarily rejected Sarah's attempt to prove the existence of God, he invited her to try again, "for I have promised myself that you are a thinker."[156] Religion and theology were subjects in which Frederick had little interest.

Sarah's restriction of subjects of their discourse was substantial but unarticulated. She almost certainly did not permit Frederick to read her notebook writings, particularly those with page references to passages in *Free Institutions 2d*. Always eager to know what she thought of his works, he would have probed those references with unwelcome persistence. There is no indication, moreover, that he ever saw her letters to Deroin and Smith, or that she ever otherwise shared with him her vision of educated women as spiritual mentors, which those two letters expounded. And although there are hints of it in her notebook writings – all almost certainly created after the August 4, 1856 Smith letter (the later of the two) – Sarah's notebooks themselves contain nothing approaching those letters' explicit portrayal of the spiritual cosmography of women's future "sphere."

That she was not ready freely to share her perception of that sphere with Frederick is at least a plausible explanation for what appears to have been her deliberate choice to respond to his pointed request for her views on his conclusions in *Rights of Women,* by a letter that would cross in the mail with his year-end, 1859 visit. She must have known almost to the day when to expect the visit, which would have required preparations in the Weld household. Telling Frederick that she had already given her response in a letter he would receive when he returned home might have helped her avoid uncomfortable discussion of the subject during his visit. Speculation that Sarah might have been holding back from fully sharing her thoughts on the future of educated American women is also encouraged by a comment her friend and first biographer Catherine Birney once made, on experiencing another instance of Sarah's reserve. "Her ideal of education was very high," Birney wrote in her biography of the sisters, "and contemplated an education *so different from the usual one, that she seldom ventured to unfold it"* [italics added].[157]

It is apparent, in any case, that Sarah's letter gave Frederick little to go on when he tried to sum up her views. Continuing in his December 14, 1859 reply, he wrote:

> The case of women who have not married will form
> an exception . . . because having no family, domestic
> life cannot be considered as exclusively or chiefly
> their destination. But if we say as a general rule that
> women may enter any of the professions like men,
> we establish two contrary rules, one which insists
> that domestic life is their appropriate destination,
> and another which must constantly, and materially
> interferes with that destination.

This observation is strikingly similar to a statement of the same contradiction by a modern scholar, one of the most insightful interpreters of Sarah's feminist thought. In a work published in 1994, Elizabeth Ann Bartlett wrote of Sarah's struggle in her early work, *Letters on the Equality of the Sexes,* "between the notion that men and women are equal in every respect and the notion that women have a special destiny to fulfill, separate from that or men; between the need boldly to mark out new worlds for women and the need to assure women of their worth as wives and mothers." Synthesizing from a perspective that included some of Sarah's later works, Professor Bartlett found, as "a truer conception of [Sarah] Grimké's concept of dual roles, not overlapping spheres, but a suprasphere for women that encompasses all of men's roles as well as sets aside specific functions and roles as the special province of woman." Explicit descriptions of Sarah's vision of woman as man's spiritual mentor set forth in her Deroin and Smith letters, of which Bartlett, not citing them, was perhaps unaware, reinforce Bartlett's conception of Sarah's placement of educated women in an all-encompassing "suprasphere" – a status which Bartlett equates to today's "superwoman."[158]

Especially noteworthy is Frederick's segue into another topic. His response to whatever Sarah said about his essay concluded with:

> But I must leave this, for another subject, <u>which interests you even more closely</u>. You mentioned that Judge O'Neal had written reminiscences . . . of our brothers, as well as of our Father . . . [underscoring added]

This December 14, 1859 letter of Frederick's is his last known communication with Sarah about *Rights of Women in a Democratic Republic*, or its prediction of the future of educated American women. Subsequent letters now in the Weld-Grimké archive, all warmly affectionate, concerned family matters, reminiscences, golden memories, and his recommendations of books he thought she and Angelina should read. Neither Frederick nor Sarah took any further action to have *Rights of Women* published during his lifetime. Darkening prospects of sectional conflict over slavery took much of his attention. His visit to Eagleswood late in 1859 was the last occasion of his seeing the sisters.

By a new will executed September 1, 1862 he qualified directions he had previously given for the essay's posthumous publication, stating that "as it stands, it may excite dissension, and suggest new views, which constitute one half the merit of the composition," while noting his "desire to alter [it] materially." But Frederick never made any such alteration. His next and final action respecting the work was to attach a note to the manuscript, directing that it not be published at all.

Epilogue: How *Rights of Women* Was Saved

"Copperheads": Democrats who opposed the federal government's use of force against southern states' secession, were especially numerous in southern Ohio.[159] In 1863, when public assertions of that opposition had begun to interfere with the Union war effort by encouraging draft resistance and desertion, General Ambrose Burnside, commander of the Ohio military district, ordered the arrest of the Copperheads' outspoken leader, Clement Vallandigham. Charged for giving an anti-war speech alleged to violate Burnside's order against "the habit of declaring sympathies for the enemy," he was arrested by soldiers who forcibly entered his Dayton, Ohio home on the night of March 5, 1863. Put on trial the following day before a military commission, he was convicted a day later, on March 7th, and sentenced to imprisonment for the duration of the war. News of these proceedings incited mob violence, and offices of leading Ohio newspapers on both sides of the controversy were trashed.[160]

It was thus at the nadir of his hopes for peaceful separation of the southern states that on the next day, Sunday, March 8, 1863, Frederick Grimke died. "His death was painless and gradual," Sarah wrote to one of the Weld children when she received the news from Chillicothe, "and he passed away in a sweet sleep." After recounting approvingly terms of his will providing bequests to Angelina and their sister Mary Ann (Grimké) Frost, and the provision for posthumous publication of this works, Sarah added:

> *We [she and Angelina] had written to him repeatedly urging him to tell us how he was after we heard of "the stricture of the throat" which troubled him but he never wrote again and doubtless this arose from his unselfishness. He knew one of us would immediately have gone to him had we known his situation and he wished to spare us such a journey at this season. This is a sweet consoling reflection but it seems very sad to have him die in a Hotel without one sister to soothe him.*[161]

Summoned from Columbus where as a prominent leader of the Ohio Democratic party he was at the vortex of the turmoil which followed Vallandigham's arrest, Frederick's friend and executor Allen G. Thurman took charge of arrangements for services and burial. The local newspaper's obituary lauded Frederick as "a sound thinker and a forcible and perspicuous writer," and reported in detail the provision in his will for publication of his works.[162] Longer remembered by some of the townspeople were instructions he had given the staff of the Valley House, the hotel where he resided, when he pointed out the suit of clothes in which he wished to be buried. "They are to be well aired before you put me in them," he ordered."[163] Burial was in Chillicothe's aptly named Grandview Cemetery, in a lot with the grandest view of all – a vista uncluttered by any work of human fabrication, looking southeast, across a deep valley. The simple monument Thurman ordered has only Frederick's name, and the dates and places of his birth and death.

The two had been close, and their friendship was built on relationships of long standing. Born in Virginia in 1813, Thurman was two years old when his family moved to Ohio and settled in Chillicothe; he was seven when Frederick arrived there in 1820. His mother, one the few Chillicothe women acquaintances mentioned in Frederick's writings, ran a school for youngsters in which her son, Allen, was a pupil. Years later in a letter to Sarah, Frederick cited "a fine remark of Mrs. Thurman of this town, who upon being asked, how she had found time amidst the avocations of a family, and of keeping school, to amass such an abundance of information, answered, that it was by regulating her time."[164] As Allen grew up in Chillicothe he would have known, or known about, Frederick as a common pleas judge. And later, after studying law in an uncle, William Allen's office and gaining admission to the bar, Thurman would likely have had some contact with Frederick as a judge of the Ohio Supreme Court. Thurman's own career in public office began with his election to the U.S. House of Representatives in 1844, after he had moved to Columbus. Returning there after serving one term in Congress, he became a prominent member of the Ohio bar. Elected in 1852 to the Ohio Supreme Court, he served on its bench for four years, the latter part of that time as Chief Justice. As a leader of Ohio Democrats he supported Stephen A. Douglas's candidacy in the 1860 Presidential election.

Despite extensive involvement with the turbulent affairs of his party during the Civil War, Thurman administered Frederick's estate with remarkable diligence. Most of its modest value was in income-producing third-party notes that Frederick's Cincinnati friend William Greene had conveyed to him in 1856. The transaction was effectively a gift, but probably at Frederick's insistence it had been given the form of a *quid pro quo*: his assigning to Greene the copyright in *Free Institutions* in exchange for Greene's transferring the notes. Liquidating them to pay the bequests to sisters Angelina and Mary Ann Frost and fund Frederick's appropriation of two thousand dollars to be used for posthumous publication of his works, along with getting Greene to give back the copyright to permit *Free Institutions* to be featured in that publication, were tasks that made great demands on Thurman's time, and he performed them without compensation. By April, 1865, the month of Lee's surrender at Appomattox, Thurman had liquidated the notes, settled with Greene, paid the legacies, funded the will's appropriation of publication money, and delivered Frederick's personal effects to designated recipients, thus completing the estate's probate administration. The accounting filed with the probate court included his receipt for the two thousand dollars publication money, which Thurman himself was to hold as trustee for that use.[165]

He had been careful to avoid Vallandigham's fate. In June, 1863, three months after Frederick's death, General Burnside issued another directive, General Order No. 87, which prohibited publication of "disloyal" books. "What is a disloyal book in his estimation," Thurman wrote to Angelina two months later, "of course nobody knows." But since *Free Institutions* contained a chapter in which Frederick had argued that states had a constitutional right to secede, and his miscellaneous writings included a letter pleading for their being allowed to go peacefully, Thurman had "not thought it prudent to begin the publication yet."[166]

In January, 1866, with the war over and the probate estate settled, another difficulty arose: the amount Thurman held as trustee was insufficient to fund the publication. "Your brother's works are not in press," he reported to Angelina. "Since it was possible to publish them without interference [from such as General Burnside] I have sought both here [in Columbus] and at Cincinnati to find a publisher, but have met with no one who would undertake, at this time, to print an edition in suitable style, for the fund in my hands."[167] One wonders why at this point Thurman did not seek the sisters' consent and the court's permission to abandon the project. None of his letters reflects anything coming back from Sarah or Angelina in the way of enthusiasm for implementing Frederick's wish to have a posthumous edition of his works; they would hardly have welcomed being publicly associated with a book expounding secessionist and pro-slavery views; and Angelina could well have used the two thousand dollars that would have gone over to her as Frederick's residuary beneficiary. But the sisters apparently said nothing. Thurman decided to invest the money at interest, and wait.[168]

Political developments affecting his public career would make his continuing fidelity to the publication project especially remarkable. Ohio Democrats during the Reconstruction era were, as Professor Robert Sawrey puts it, "a minority desperately seeking issues with which to return to power," and in that quest they "resorted to some of the most vicious race baiting in all American history."[169] After their legislative office holders voted as a minority in the Ohio General Assembly to oppose ratification of the 13th and 14th amendments (the 13th abolished slavery, the 14th made the federal constitution's bill of rights applicable to the states), the Democrats rode the unpopularity of a Republican-sponsored ballot measure to eliminate "white" as an Ohio constitution's voter qualification, to gain a victory in 1867 state elections which gave them temporary control of both legislative houses and nearly won them the governorship. Thurman himself was their candidate for that office, and he came within two thousand votes of defeating Rutherford B. Hayes, a Republican with a good war record. But whatever was Thurman's disappointment over losing the governorship, it was assuaged by the Ohio legislature temporarily under his party's control, when in 1869 it elected him to the U.S. Senate (whose members were then chosen by state legislatures). Other actions of the same Democrat-controlled legislature: to rescind Ohio's ratification of the 14th amendment, and decline ratification of the 15th (prohibiting states from denying the right to vote on account of race), were subsequently nullified by the 14th's purported rescission being ignored by federal authorities, and 15th amendment's being ratified by the next legislature after the fall, 1869 elections gave the Republicans effective control of both houses.[170]

With his election to the U.S. Senate Thurman began what would become a distinguished career in national political affairs, extending through two six-year terms. By 1871, when Frederick's *Works* were finally published, Thurman's political base had undergone a fundamental reorientation. Turning away from a platform epitomized by a slogan first proclaimed in 1863, "the Constitution as it is, the Union as it was, and the negroes where they are," Ohio Democrats proclaimed a "new departure," acknowledging the post-Civil War Constitutional amendments as the law of the land, and redirecting their partisan efforts to focus on economic issues.[171] Any perceived identification with views Frederick had asserted in *Free Institutions,* defending the constitutional legitimacy of secession and urging toleration of black slavery in the South, would have been seriously harmful to Thurman's standing at this time with Ohio voters of any political affiliation.

It is not surprising, then, that Thurman's name nowhere appears in the two cheaply fabricated volumes bound within a single set of book covers, which the Columbus Printing Company finally produced in 1871 as *The Works of Frederick Grimke.* In an unsigned "Publisher's Preface," which began with three paragraphs recounting Frederick's life, Thurman went on to state:

> It is no part of the purpose of this notice to review these productions. Some of the author's views were, when published, unpopular, and are now yet more so; but he was not a man to be deterred from expressing his honest convictions . . . .
>
> To those who personally knew him . . . his memory is endeared by a recollection of his unassuming manners, his kindness of heart, and the purity of life unstained by a blot.

The two volumes are separately identified only by title pages; neither has a table of contents. The first volume with the greater number of pages was the third edition of Frederick's treatise, *The Nature and Tendency of Free Institutions;* the second contained miscellaneous writings, the last of which is *The Rights of Women in a Democratic Republic.*[172] Since the Columbus Printing Company was also printer for *The Crisis,* Ohio's principal Democratic newspaper with a large circulation in the state capital, one wonders whether Thurman had to call in a favor in order to get the printing done for the funds he had in hand. He also used the paper's editor and publisher, Dr. William Trevitt, an old political ally, to front distribution of the posthumous *Works* edition pursuant to a direction

126

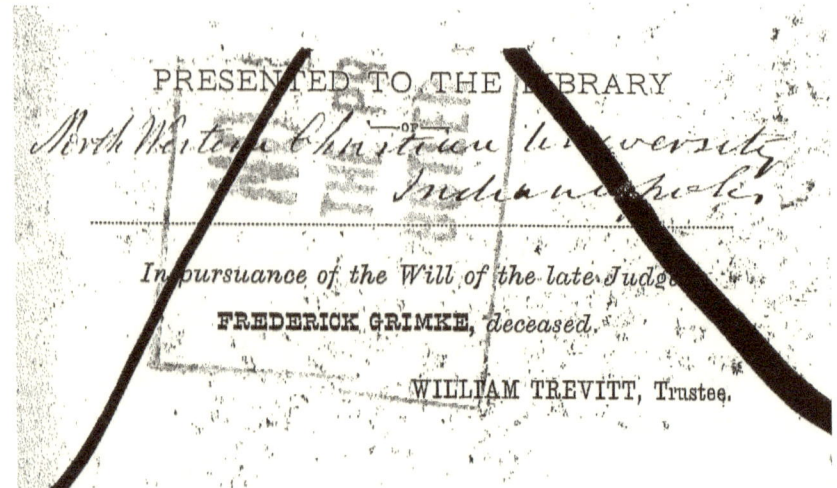

Illustration 12. Presentation book plate: North Western Christian University (now Butler University), Indianapolis, Indiana, of the copy of the third edition of Frederick Grimke's *WorksKappa* presently owned by the author of this Commentary. Marks indicate subsequent de-accessioning by Butler University library.

in Frederick's will that copies be given "to the Congressional libraries of the U. States, and the Confederate States, to each of the state libraries and to the chief college in each." The presentation copies carried bookplates memorializing the gift, as implemented by Trevitt as "trustee." The bookplate exhibited here from the copy now owned by the author was presented to a newly founded institution in Indianapolis, subsequently renamed and presently existing as Butler University, which coincidentally had just become, in 1869, the first university in the United States to endow a chair designated specifically for a woman.[173] Presentations to designated institutions might have been the *Works*' only distribution; there is no indication of any commercial sale.[174]

But the *Works'* major component, Frederick's *Free Institutions* treatise, had another posthumous edition – an unauthorized Spanish translation with a respectable sale of copies, published in 1870 by Florentino Gonzalez, a veteran of South American revolutionary struggles.[175] Caught up in political ferment and held for a time under sentence of death for alleged complicity in a plot to assassinate Simon Bolivar when the latter's regime became dictatorial, Gonzalez subsequently entered academic life, and from 1833 to 1839, had been professor of constitutional rights, administrative sciences and international law in the University of Bogota. Having cited *Free Institutions'* first edition in his own writings advocating democratic rule and public education, he evidently thought highly enough of the application of Frederick's teachings to the new South American republics to undertake the laborious effort of translating the work into Spanish. There is no indication of how Gonzalez came upon it, or that he was aware of any subsequent edition. In the introduction to his translation he hailed "the American from Cincinnati" (the place of the first edition's publication) for articulating a "science of republicanism based on deduced principles, not abstract ideas of the imagination."[176] His explanation for the scarcity of the original edition's copies would have pleased Frederick: Gonzalez imagined that *Free Institutions* had been so "avidly read" in the United States that the supply "was exhausted."[177] Republished in subsequent editions, the translation was "still read and continued to be of influence" in South America, as reported almost fifty years later.[178] Not mentioned in Professor Ward's introduction to the Harvard University Press's modern republication, it brought

Frederick all the readership recognition his life's work would receive, for a century following his death.

- - - -

With its placement at the end of the unorganized collection of miscellaneous writings which comprise the second volume of Frederick's *Works*, and with that volume's being bound along with the first within a single set of book covers and lacking any table of contents, it is hardly surprising that *The Rights of Women in a Democratic Republic* has been missed by compilers of research library catalogs and finding aids. But awaiting the essay's happenstance discoverer is a great curiosity. An asterisk next to its title directs attention to a footnote at the bottom of the page, which can only have been Thurman's. It sets forth Frederick's instruction not to publish the essay, and Thurman's explanation for doing so notwithstanding:

> * The following note, in pencil, in Judge Grimke's hand writing, was appended to the manuscript sheets of this essay:
>
> NOTE. – This essay is not to be published, as the views are pushed to an extreme. It is an effort to find out the truth, a preliminary investigation only. When re-written, and the views in some parts considerably modified, it will be published.
>
> The author, when he wrote this note, evidently contemplated very considerable modification of the views herein presented: and it was not till after very serious and thoughtful deliberation,

and consultations with judicious friends, that the manuscript was placed by the publisher, in the hands of the printer; it being deemed improper, that so valuable a contribution to a subject now so largely agitating the public mind, should be withheld from the world, notwithstanding that the author, if living, might desire to largely modify these views.

Thurman would have known of the essay's existence from its specific mention in Frederick's will. But with all his preoccupations, it seems quite possible that he did not see the note Frederick appended to the manuscript until much later, in 1871, when he decided to publish it. His correspondence with the sisters does not mention the essay. Indeed it is plausible to suppose that the note was first noticed by a Columbus Printing Company journeyman printer as he was about to set the essay in type. And however it might have come to Thurman's attention, one wonders why he did not simply instruct the printer to "leave it in" (or alternatively, "leave it out") and been done with it. Thurman did not owe readers of the *Works* any explanation for his decision. Indeed, his choice to include the essay might plausibly have been justified as consistent with Frederick's expressed wish, if his instruction not to publish were read as contingent on his later substituting a revised version, which he never did. Thurman left nothing else to satisfy our curiosity: in 1948 his granddaughter reported to an institutional librarian that his papers were "no longer in existence."[179]

There is nothing to suggest that he had been aware of Sarah's efforts to get *Rights of Women* published during Frederick's lifetime, or that he knew anything of her and Frederick's subsequent deliberations over its conclusions. The sisters never came to Ohio, and their public lives had practically ended before Frederick's death. If Thurman had any awareness of their connection with the women's rights movement, it wasn't enough to have been reflected in his correspondence with them. As to the "judicious friends" Thurman said he consulted – well, American politicians have lots of "friends," and perhaps he partook of their habit of calling on them rhetorically to create an appearance of support for a position.

A more substantive element of Thurman's explanation for including the essay is his characterizing it as "a contribution to a subject now so largely agitating the public mind." In 1871, with respect to women's rights, that subject was suffrage: the demand on which the feminist movement came to focus after the Civil War. In that era, well informed Americans would likely have taken the words of the essay's title, "the rights of women in a democratic republic," to refer to women's claim to political, not occupational or economic, equality. So it seems possible, even plausible, to suppose that if he hadn't read it, Thurman would have thought that was what *Rights of Women* was about. The hypothesis is especially plausible if his decision to publish the essay was made while he was in Washington. The manuscript the printer had is likely to have been the only surviving copy, and if he had supposed that that Thurman had already read it, he might not have sent it to him.

But even if Thurman never read *Rights of Women* and fundamentally mistook what it was about, that wouldn't completely account for his decision to publish it. Thurman certainly knew what Frederick's *chef d'oeuvre, Free Institutions,* was about. He had read the treatise in an earlier edition, and was familiar with its conclusions – both with those that had already become embarrassing anachronisms, and with those, deeply insightful, that have enduring value. Indeed it's hard to think of anything else that would account for the tenacity with which Thurman pursued the project for posthumous publication of Frederick's works. In particular, he would have been fascinated with Frederick's perception of the effect of extending the franchise to groups who had never before enjoyed the right to vote, that

> . . . every enlargement of it increases the demand [to further extend the right] by raising up a greater number of people who are fitted to exercise it. The improvement of the political institutions and the improvement of the population go hand in hand.[180]

We will never know whether that is what Allen Granberry Thurman actually had in mind when he acted to include *The Rights of Women in a Democratic Republic* in the literary legacy that his friend Frederick Grimke had given him to preserve. But there is a delightful reflection of the thought showing up obliquely in Thurman's later career.

After his rise to national prominence while serving two terms in the United States Senate, he ultimately became a candidate for another high political office. Well-liked and respected by Senate colleagues in both parties, Thurman had been instrumental in the resolution of an Electoral College impasse over disputed returns in the 1876 Presidential election, by an Electoral Commission he helped create, and on which he sat, which ruled by a one-vote majority to award the victory to his former Ohio gubernatorial opponent Rutherford Hayes, thus depriving New York Democrat Samuel B. Tilden of his win of the popular vote. Ironically Thurman himself would experience that deprivation in the 1888 Presidential election, as Grover Cleveland's Vice-Presidential running mate on a ticket which also gained a popular vote majority but suffered an uncontroverted Electoral College loss.[181]

Looking for a souvenir of that culminating event of Thurman's political career, I found this cartoon in *Puck*, a magazine of political satire published from 1871 to 1918.[182] The message was serious: in a Presidential election voters should disregard local political squabbles and focus on issues of national importance, in this case the tariff, a nineteenth-century perennial. But it's the depiction of participants in those squabbles that delights, for it shows what Frederick predicted about the extension of the franchise, "even to the extreme into which the people of the United States have run, of introducing universal suffrage, or nearly so":

> The natural and the legal majority being rendered identical, *the surface of society is frequently ruffled,* but the existence of the institution is no longer jeopardized [emphasis supplied].[183]

Here many of the surface-rufflers are from groups, including recent immigrants, new to the experience of voting in U.S. elections. Tammany Hall and other Democrat factions are in the fray, along with Socialists. The brandisher of the multicultural "**Vas is Lost Mit Coogan**" sign adds an appearance of oriental heritage to that diverse combination.

Illustration 13. "A Plain Duty," *Puck*, Oct. 31, 1888.

And at the back of the crowd, with only the bearer's distinctively feminine headgear showing, is a sign reading:

> ### Cynthia Leonard for Mayor
> ### Women's Rights

American women had arrived in the political arena. They belonged in the picture.

APPENDICES

President Dwight's
Decisions of Questions
Discussed by
The Senior Class in Yale College
in 1813 and 1814

from Stenographic Notes
by Theodore Dwight, Jun.

New York:
Nathan Leavitt, 182 Broadway
Boston: Crocker & Brewster, 47 Washington St.
1833

- - - -

Dispute VI
November 17, 1813

Question: Are the Abilities of the Sexes Equal?

Remark 1ˢᵗ. The mother gives the first turn and cast to the mind. Her province is infinitely more valuable than that of the father. General Washington's mother contributed to the foundation of his character. Sir William Jones's mother performed the same important part in the education of her son.

Remark 2d. Mrs. Hanah More has written better on the human character, than any man whose writings I have seen. Her treatise on female education is far superior to that of Mr. Locke, as his is to that of an ordinary man. Her system of morals is the best in the world.

Remark 3d. It does not appear that bodily and mental strength go parallel. I have seen many strong men with strong minds; but I have seen men who were strong in mind, but weak in body. Dr.Johnson was strong it is true. He knocked down a bookseller with a book. Governor Strong of Massachusetts could probably be outrun by most of the butchers in the state.

Decision

There can be no decision on this subject, because the different manner of educating the different sexes deprives us of facts. Mr. Kirkland, a missionary to the Indians, informed me, that one of the Iroquois tribes had a woman who was considered the most able counsellor among them.

It is owing to the innate good sense of the women of this country, that they are not absolute idiots. I would not give three groats to have a daughter of mine go to many of the schools in the country. Observe the state of our schools for females, and compare them with the colleges for males. The seminaries for females are no better than hired school rooms; and how disproportioned are the benefits of instruction offered in the two plans of instruction? Yet under all theses advantages in the one case, and disadvantages in the other, we are comparing the abilities of the sexes. The end kept in view in our institutions for the education of males, is to make them useful: in that of females, to make them admired. Men will pay anything to have their daughters taught to manage their feet in dancing, to daub over a few pictures, &c. to be admired by a few silly young men. I cannot speak on this subject without indignation.

In spite of all the disadvantages under which they suffer, females have not only become good, (which they have done oftener than men,) but great. Elizabeth was better than any sovereign that ever sat on the English throne, except Alfred the Great. Catharine of Russia, though in some respects bad, was better than the other monarchs of that country. Margaret of Denmark was great. Women on thrones have generally excelled men in that station. What a miserable collection of kings have set on the thrones of England, France, Spain, and other countries of Europe! It has been said that Elizabeth's character is due to the wisdom of her ministers. Their wisdom only shows that she had sagacity enough to choose such ministers. In literature woman can appear to great advantage. No writer has equaled Mrs. More on the subjects she has handled.

In determining this question we are prone to be prejudiced. We are like the man who showed a lion a statue of a man treading upon a lion's neck, to prove to him the superiority of his own species. "Ah," said the lion, "let us be painters, and we will soon show you a lion with a man at his feet."

But females excel us in moral excellence. In comparison with this, even good sense and enlarged intelligence are mere frippery. Women are much more frequently persons of piety than men. Their dependent situation is favorable to it. It may be set down as a strong probability that many more women than men will to go heaven.

Appendix B

Thomas Grimké, "Female Education"

An essay published posthumously in a newspaper,
by his sisters Angelina and Sarah.
In form a letter, the intended addressee as well as the newspaper's
identity are unknown. The essay survives
only as a clipping in the Weld-Grimké archive's miscellany.
A news article on the reverse side indicates a
January, 1836 publication date.

Text markings here indicate deletions in the
portion Sarah Grimké quoted, in
Letter VIII of her *Letters on the Equality of the
Sexes and the Condition of Woman*
(1838), repr. Elizabeth Ann Bartlett, ed, *Sarah Grimké Letters
on the Equality of the Sexes and Other Essays*
(New Haven: Yale Univ. Press, 1988)

- - - -

Female Education

[Note by the sisters] The following letter on Female Education from the pen of Thomas S. Grimke has never before been published.

I return the No. of the Museum and thank you for the opportunity of reading the article from the Westminster Review. I agree with the writer entirely in the high estimate which he places on female education, and have long since been satisfied that the subject not only merits but imperiously demands a thorough consideration. The whole scheme must, in my opinion, be reconstructed. The great elements of duty and usefulness are too little attended to, and scraps and fragments of reading, writing, arithmetic, and perhaps French, occupy nearly one-half the time, while fashion seizes the other. Women ought, in my view of the subject, to approach to the best education now given to men (I except mathematics and the classics,) far more, I believe. than has ever yet been attempted. ~~After excluding the branches which I have just mentioned, and others perfectly manly, such as public speaking and political studies, or purely professional, as Law, Medicine and Divinity, should not a woman be educated in every other aspect like a man? With the exceptions just made, I know nothing that I would teach to man, that I would not teach to woman. And this I should do, not only because women ought to be educated as refined and intelligent companions for men, but chiefly because women actually exercise as mothers and sisters and teachers, a much greater influence over the minds and characters of children of both sexes, through the whole period of childhood and youth, than men do as fathers and brothers, and teachers. Educated women will make educated men, but educated men never will make educated women.~~ Give me a host of educated, pious mothers and sisters, and I will no more to revolutionize a country in moral and religious taste, and in manners, social virtues and intellectual cultivation, than I possibly could do in double or treble the time, with a similar host of educated men. I cannot but think that the miserable condition of the great body of the people in all the ancient communities is to be ascribed in a very large degree, to the degradation of women. Show me among the modern nations, those in which women exercise the least influence in domestic and social circles, and I instance Spain and Portugal, and I will show you a people dishonored by ignorance and afflicted by oppression. Show me, on the other hand a country in which the mother, the wife, the sister, and the daughter have exercised the greatest influence in the development and formation of the male and female character, and I will show you the freest, happiest, and most enlightened of nations, our own fortunate and favored land. And what a remarkable illustration do we find in France, emphatically the Empire of Women, but of woman, a freethinker, the idol of flattery, the devotee of fashion, faithless, dissolute, and heartless. Educated woman has there been a curse, instead of a blessing, because she was trained up to immorality and hypocrisy, to be flattered, not respected, to be admired rather than beloved.

[For myself, I cannot express too strongly and earnestly my deep sense of the value of female education: not that of which would make a man-woman like Madame De Stael; but of that which would fill our land with such women as Hannah More, Mrs. Barbauld, Mrs. Trimmer, and all their admirable compatriot worthies. I think, if I ever write again for the Southern Review, I should delight to make this the subject. Let me not be understood as objecting to such women as Madame De Stael, provided the number be small, for a few only of such intellectual heroines, the Marphesas, and the Bradamants of literary and intellectual chivalry, are important to vindicate the power and glory of the sex against the false and ungenerous aspersions of inferiority. Such a charge comes from that sex which cannot produce, in proportion to their numbers and advantages, as many of the illustrious in arts and arms, as the other sex, the object of their contumely and ridicule. It comes with an ill grace from that sex which has so often been ruled and molded to their will, by such women of the ancient world, as Semiramis, Zenobia, and Amalasonta, and by such in the modern, as Elizabeth, Margaret, and the Catharines of Russia.]*

T. S. G.

* Bracketed portion also omitted from Sarah's quotation in her Letter VIII, *Letters on the Equality of the Sexes.*

Appendix C

Letter of Sarah M. Grimké to "Her Friend" Gerrit Smith
originally published in *The Lily* 8, no. 19 (Oct. 1, 1856)

Eagleswood School, August 4th [1856]

Dear Gerrit:

The subject of your letter to E. C. Stanton has often claimed my serious consideration. It treats of points of vital interest to humanity; points the right view of which is essential to the progress of our cause. I rejoice that you wrote it, not because I accede to all the positions you assume, but because I hope it may awaken thought, lead women to study themselves, to understand their relation to the world, and quicken their perception of the fact that whatever form of dress their taste, judgment and good sense may approve, they are bound as Reformers to let that dress be simple, uncostly, convenient and healthy.

I must confess that the Reform dress offends my taste; but its manifest fitness for walking in the country, through bushes and brakes, jumping fences, working in the garden, and all sorts of domestic labor, is an appeal to common sense which I cannot resist. I therefore wear it for all such purposes, but I see no reason why it should be worn when seated quietly at home, or passing about a city, any more than a farmer who is visiting his friends or spending a few days in New York should wear his working clothes or appear in the parlor in his shirt sleeves. Appropriateness ought to govern dress, and the moderately long dress appears to me most appropriate in the city, except when one is engaged in domestic business, or when the walking is wet.

It is not, however, the form of dress among women which pains me, as much as the ministration through it to their lower nature – to vanity, to love of admiration, to the spirit of extravagance. It strikes me that all you say respecting the dress of woman, leads to the conclusion that she cannot enjoy true freedom and independence unless her dress leaves her limbs as free to move as possible, at the same time you insist on a distinction in dress.

Now, it is perfectly clear to me that the position, relations, duties, circumstances, avocations of woman do not demand such a dress at all times – that she could wear it constantly at the sacrifice of feeling, delicacy and convenience. Here and there you may find a Helen Weber or a Captain Betsy Smith. If they have chosen professions which render any womanly dress incommodious and improper, I have nothing to say. Let them follow out the proclivities of their peculiar natures; but I cannot believe that those professions, or many others, such as house and ship building, and all the rougher and more laborious occupations belong to woman, or that she will ever follow them to any extent.

True there are many kinds of businesses that both sexes may engage in; many of the handicraft trades are of this description, and I rejoice that women are gradually introducing themselves into employments from which they have hitherto been excluded, such as the offices of clerk, salesman, bookkeeper, &c. This more extensive range of business relations, of contact with men, will operate most favorably; it cannot but produce a wider scope for thought, a greater opportunity for intellectual activity, a larger circumference of action, sharpen the powers of invention, increase the desire for usefulness and independence, and enable woman to take more comprehensive views of everything respecting herself, her relations to the whole human family, and the co-relation of one thing to another. But enough of this. The next generation will produce women of higher organization, of finer intellectual and moral development; they will not worship at the shrine of fashion, or allow themselves to be cheated of their common sense, their health, their convenience. They will realize what the Poet says:

> Life is real, life is earnest,
> Let us then be up and doing,
> With a heart for any fate;
> Still achieving, still pursuing,
> Learn to labor and to wait,

Meanwhile, although the present laborers in the cause of human rights may fall short of our ideal of Reformers, yet let us heartily accord to them both gratitude and praise. They have done a mighty work. It is by posterity that the present attempt to gain the rights which appertain to humanity will be estimated, and the high value of the social speculation now made be appreciated. They may be destined to failures in our generation, but they furnish the light which will guide to the ultimate settlement of the great question – "The execution of their design may be far from corresponding to the greatness of the enterprise, but no failure in the carrying out can impair the value of the conception."

I entirely dissent, my dear friend, from your affirmation that the"Woman's Rights Movement is not in the right hands." Surely you must admit that many of the noblest, most independent, most morally exalted, most highly cultivated, most comprehensive minds are engaged in this reform – that the most vain, the most heartless, the most frivolous, the least cultivated intellectually, and developed spiritually, stand aloof from our ranks. "It cannot now be necessary to prove that ideas govern the world, or throw it into chaos. In other words, that all social mechanism rests upon opinion."

Now the past history of woman clearly proves that she has been regarded as a slave, or the plaything of man, a being *created for him*, created mainly to minister to his material comfort, to surrender herself to the gratification of his passions and appetites – at one time the object of his silly adoration, at another the machine which moved at his bidding, run [sic] in his grooves, and worked for his advantage – not exclusively, to be sure, for God has so arranged social and domestic life; that whatever we do for the happiness and welfare of others, always contributes to our own. Since the creation of woman, this has been her experience, her education, her discipline. Could she be other than she is? What is there in her pupilage to develop her intellect, to train her mind, to excite her to independence in thought, or in action? But it was not the opinion of man respecting woman, not his treatment of her that most powerfully tended to render her imbecile, contriving, dependent, effeminate, willing to live on *his* earnings, and recline in his bowers. The debasement was infinitely more the result of her accepting his opinions as Truth, and thus losing her self-respect. But could she in her then stage of development do otherwise? Surely not; she naturally regarded him as her superior, loved her ease, hugged her chains, nor asked a better state. But the time has came [sic] when physical force and intellectual acumen have wrought until they are weary. Man begins to perceive that he possesses a spiritual nature of which he had hardly been cognizant, which demands nutriment of another kind, enjoyments of a higher order, incitements and exercise of a superior quality. He begins, too, to perceive that while *he* has been pursuing animal gratifications and reveling in the fields of literature and science, Woman's love nature had been unfolding and strengthening, and becoming more and more under the elevating influence of reason - that in her social and domestic relations she exhibits more tenderness, more patient watchfulness, more power of endurance, and that the exercise of these affections has called forth a higher spirituality, a greater devotion to God, a more intimate acquaintance with Christ, a stronger lover for the truths of religion, a closer adherence to its precepts than has marked his character. Hence he begins to look to woman as the channel through which his higher, his spiritual self may receive the nourishment he craves. From her he had drawn the elixir of animal life – from her he received the first look of affection, the first tear of sympathy, the first smile of approval. Her arms had been his cradle and his shield – on her bosom he found a cradle of repose.

Do we wonder that he turns to her to find spiritually what he had found materially? Shall he turn in vain? The holiest instincts of her nature answers [sic] no.

Man, in acknowledging the superiority of woman's religious nature, her greater attainments in the inner life gives her the highest assurance of his co-operation in her attempt to rise from her present degradation. He feels that there is something above power and science necessary to satisfy the yearnings of his immortal soul, and that woman is the medium through which he may receive it. She asks but time and patience – can we deny them to her?

When we remember what the condition of woman has been, how all her educational discipline has been calculated to check her aspirations after intellectual development which render man intelligent, comprehensive, far seeing, wise to plan, strong to execute and willing to endure toil to secure independence, we may marvel that there is as much left out of which to realize "Woman as she will be." Her "tendency to improvement must be highly spontaneous and irresistible, to have enabled her to persevere, notwithstanding the enormous faults which have at all times absorbed or neutralized" her life forces. The fact that she has been no more deteriorated by all the appliances [sic] to her lower nature, by all the drawbacks to her higher, inspires not merely a hope, but a faith that she will yet be the savior of the world in conjunction with man, under the guidance and inspiration of their common Father.

Thus regarding woman, I cannot but believe that her cause is in the right hands. She must do the work of elevation herself. No power out of herself can do it for her. There is a period in all reforms when, as Guizot well observes, "Men *will* feebly, but *desire* immensely;" and if woman has come to this mighty conflict partly shorn of her strength, by her love of dress, by her puerile passion for ornament and display, let us not forget that as an intellectual being she is in her childhood or adolescence. Let us accept her for what she is, for what she must inevitably be from habit, surroundings and education, until she learns by experience what kind of woman the age calls for, and bends her powers to become what is needed. I have no fears for the success of this divinely inspired reform. My confidence in the moral endowments of my sex and in their love of humanity is unbounded. I know they are capable of great self-sacrifice, of noble deeds, of intense suffering. I know that for this cause they had endured reproach, contumely, scorn, derision - they will endure more, and they will conquer. They will offer their vanity as a whole burnt offering on the altar of "Human Rights."

Let us have patience with the present, it is the mother of a better future, and that future will usher in a yet more glorious day. "God hath chosen the weak things of the world to confound the things which are mighty, and base things of the world, and things which are despised, hath God chosen, yea, and things which are not to bring to nought things that are."

The philosopher who has perhaps reflected more deeply than any other on the history of the human race, says: "Experience alone can teach us the measure of our powers. If men did not begin by an exaggerated estimate of what they can do, they would never have done all that they are capable of. Our organization requires this." Woman, under the strong feeling that she is deprived of her rights as a human being, may have made an over-estimate of her capabilities, but as no force, however intense, can effect any modification in society which is not in accordance with the necessities of the age, nothing will be lost by this over-estimate. The very fact that her claims are high will stimulate her to aim at becoming fit to meet the responsibilities and duties which belong to the elevated position to which she aspires. She is now receiving an education, passing through a discipline which she needs, and which she can only gain by a severe experience. She is acquiring knowledge which will make her see the necessity of thinking and acting for herself, undergoing an ordeal which will teach her to prize self-reliance, gaining an independence which will teach her to pursue some occupation that will secure a maintenance to herself and enable her to aid in the support of her family. There are multitudes of women whose energies are frittered away in the little occupations of domestic life, who might and would do all they now do, and turn the residue of their time to useful account, if they had some employment which was remunerative. The time, I trust is not far distant when it will be regarded as humiliating to be dependent on a father, husband, brother, cousin, &c, unless circumstances absolutely disqualify a woman from earning her own living. Custom has rendered dependence so common that it really *seems* right; but men are beginning to weary of this double burden, and one who remarked that he should rejoice to see the waste time in his family turned to some profitable account, only spoke the feelings of thousands whose premature wrinkles and care work faces proclaim that their strength is overtasked.

I cannot but hope that this appeal to the heart of woman will operate to rouse her to a sense of her obligations to do what she can towards supplying her own material wants, and this will unquestionably open to her the means of ministering to those of her intellectual nature. When she encounters the path of usefulness and duty, she cannot but see the incompatibility of her present dress with true womanly dignity. I look with certainty to the time when her gewgaws and fashions will drop off as did the sword of William Penn, so soon as he was willing to part with it.

You lay down another proposition, my dear friend, which I think is wholly untenable, viz the identity of man and woman. If they are essentially the same, whence comes the difference between them? Why has man, in all ages and in all nations, exhibited more physical strength, more intellectual power, more mental endurance, more continuity of thought, more comprehensiveness, more concentration, more invention, &c., than woman? Why has she, too, her peculiarities as strongly marked as man? She has more vivacity, more sparkle, more cheerfulness, more elasticity, more quickness of apprehension, more disinterestedness, a keener sense of justice, a greater intensity of love, a higher appreciation of spiritual things. – Difference, however, does not necessarily imply superiority in either. Each has improved the faculties bestowed, and the sexes are admirably adapted to draw out and educate the distinctive characteristics of each. It seems to me that we disparage God's work by supposing that he has created two beings identically the same, instead of giving to each peculiar qualities, whereby they might mutually instruct and benefit each other. But although I assert an essential difference between the sexes, I admit that they have a common nature, physically, intellectually and spiritually. The two first they share with animals "which manifest most of our affective and even intellectual faculties, with mere difference of degree; a fact which no one ventures to deny at this day." But there is another nobler nature belonging to man. His distinguishing feature is reason, that faculty by which he perceives the eternal distinction between right and wrong. Here he has nothing in common with animals, this spark of divinity, this guide to perfection, is shared with God. ["]It is the anointing which is in you, which teacheth you of all things, and is truth, and no lie."

But whilst I accord to man superiority in physical strength, in all the more hardy and severe departments of the understanding, I must believe that the spiritual nature has been more highly developed in woman than in man, because it is universally conceded that the strength of the moral world lies in woman – that in her heart religion has found its home - that she is from her very organization more susceptible to spiritual impressions.

Now it is neither physical strength nor mighty intellect that will regenerate the world. It is the unfolding of our rational nature which will introduce the spirit of gentleness, forbearance and love, and render mankind a holy brotherhood. When these glorious attributes of Deity are embodied in woman's life, so far as the finite can approach the Infinite, she will shed around her a rich aroma which will permeate the moral atmosphere as the fragrance of flowers does the natural. But it holds true in this, as in every thing relating to the sexes, "Neither is the man without the woman, neither the woman without the man." The present conflict manifests the tendency of humanity towards a new social system – indefinite enough, but radically different from the old. This many be the negative era of social progress, but it is indispensable as a preparation for the advent of that change which will result in the elevation of woman, and the spiritual advancement of man.

Yours, most truly,
SARAH M. GRIMKE

Endnotes

1   Frederick Grimke, *The Rights of Women in a Democratic Republic*, 14. Its first and only earlier publication was as one of the essays included in the second volume of *The Works of Frederick Grimke* (Columbus, Ohio: Columbus Printing Co., 1871), 2:239-256. It will here sometimes be referred to as *"Rights of Women,"* and always with page references as published in this modern edition.

2   Sarah Grimké to Harriot Hunt, Feb. 1 [1857], in the Weld-Grimké Family Papers, William L. Clements Library, University of Michigan. Here cited as the "Weld-Grimké archive," it is the repository of all correspondence referred to in the instant work, unless otherwise stated.

3   That it was written on February 1, 1857 is inferred from an internal reference to another letter which had recently appeared in *The Lily*, a feminist newspaper published bi-monthly. Written by Frances Gage, a frequent *Lily* correspondent, the letter denounced Horace Greeley for asserting in a letter to a women's rights convention that "the intellectual, like the physical, capacities of Women [are] unequal in the average to those of men." Dated November 22, 1856, Greeley's letter was published in *The Lily*'s December 15, 1856 issue, number 24 of volume eight. Gage's denunciation would thus be expected to have appeared in one of *The Lily*'s next two issues - those of January 1 or January 15, 1857, numbers 1 or 2 of volume nine.

         A difficulty with this expectation is that *The Lily* is generally believed to have ceased publication at the end of December, 1856. See, e.g., Edward A. Hinck, "The Lily, 1849-1856: From Temperance to Women's Rights," in *A Voice of Their Own: The Woman Suffrage Press, 1840-1910*, ed. Martha M. Solomon (Tuscaloosa: University of Alabama Press, 1991), 30, 32. The New York Historical Society's collection of *Lily* issues, copied and circulated to research libraries on microform, concludes with the December 15, 1856 issue. But no imminent prospect of journalistic demise is reflected in that issue's year-end message to subscribers (to the contrary, the editor cited "signs of progress and success" in bidding her readers "adieu until invited again to visit your homes in the New Year 1857").

         Indeed *The Lily* continued publishing in 1857. A single copy of an April 15, 1857 issue has been found in the library of the Wisconsin Historical Society by an Internet search for which the author is greatly indebted to the University of Michigan Hatcher Graduate Library's Judith Avery. The number of that issue, number 8 of volume nine, is in sequence with regular bi-monthly *Lily* publication numerology. The two January, 1857 issues would have been numbers 1 and 2 of volume nine.

Other correspondence is consistent with 1857 as the year Sarah wrote her "Feb. 1ˢᵗ" letter. A completely dated June 28, 1857 letter from Sarah to Hunt refers to "brother's Essay" as a familiar and fairly recent subject of communication between them.

4   Harriot K. Hunt, M.D., *Glances and Glimpses; or Fifty Years Social, including Twenty Years Professional Life* (Boston: John P. Jewett and Co., 1856).

5   Sarah to Harriot Hunt, Jun. 28, 1857. To avoid tiresome and unnecessary repetition of their surname in frequent citation of their correspondence, Frederick Grimke and Sarah Grimké will be identified hereinafter as "Frederick" and "Sarah."

6   Frederick to Sarah, Apr. 22, 1857.

7   Frederick Grimke, *Considerations Upon the Nature and Tendency of Free Institutions*, 1ˢᵗ ed. (Cincinnati: H. W. Derby & Co., 1848); 2d ed. (New York: Derby & Jackson, Cincinnati: H. W. Derby & Co., 1856; 3d ed. entitled *Nature and Tendency of Free Institutions* published as volume 1 of *The Works of Frederick Grimke*, 2 vols. (Columbus: Columbus Printing Co., 1871); repr. entitled *The Nature and Tendency of Free Institutions* with an introduction by John William Ward (Cambridge: Belknap Press of Harvard University, 1968).

These four editions of Frederick Grimke's treatise, as often referred to herein, will be cited in short form, as follows:

Free Institutions (1ˢᵗ ed., 1848)
Free Institutions (2d ed., 1856), or *Free Institutions 2d*
Free Institutions (3d ed., 1871)
Free Institutions (Ward ed., 1968)

8   *Rights of Women*, 28.

9   Ibid., 22-25 passim.

10   Letter from Harriet Martineau, *Report of the Second General Convention of Friends of Woman's Rights, held at Worcester, October 15ᵗʰ and 16ᵗʰ, 1851* (New York: Fowlers and Wells, 1852), 13-16.

11   Speech of Lucy Stone, *Proceedings of the National Woman's Rights Convention, held at Cleveland, Ohio, on . . . October 5ᵗʰ, 6ᵗʰ and 7ᵗʰ, 1853* (Cleveland: Gray, Brandsley, 1854), 97.

12   *Report of the Second General Convention of Friends of Woman's Rights, held at Worcester, October 15ᵗʰ and 16ᵗʰ, 1851* (New York: Fowlers and Wells, 1852), 23.

[13] *Rights of Women,* 30.

[14] *Rights of Women,* 35.

[15] See, e.g. Gary L. Bunker, "Antebellum Caricature and the Woman's Sphere," *Journal of Women's History 3,* (Winter 1992): 6-43.

[16] "Woman and the 'Woman's Movement,'" *Putnam's Magazine,* March 1853, 279, 284, 287.

The article got a bemused response. A letter writer to *The Una,* a feminist journal to which Sarah subscribed, described it as "a smooth, delicate confection for the grown up babies of our sex . . . delightful to men whose philosophy reaches no further than the present day." *The Una,* April 1, 1853, 38-39.

[17] Frederick to Sarah, Apr. 22, 1857, Mar. 13, 1858, Jul. 30, 1859.

[18] Allen G. Thurman (Frederick's executor) to Angelina Grimké Weld, Jan. 20, 1866.

Professor Ward's attribution of an earlier loss of "Sarah's side of what must have been a rich correspondence" to the "great fire" which destroyed much of the town of Chillicothe in 1852 does not account for the loss of letters of interest here. Ward, Introduction to *Free Institutions* (Ward ed., 1968), 5, n. 6.

[19] Frederick to Sarah, Mar. 13, 1858.

[20] Frederick to Sarah, Nov. 23, 1858.

[21] Will of Frederick Grimke, executed Sept. 1, 1862, para. 1 (Ross County Ohio Probate Court Case No. 2769).

[22] Ibid., para. 10.

[23] *The Yale Biographical Dictionary of American Law,* ed. Roger K, Newman (New Haven: Yale University Press, 2009), s.vv. "John Milton Goodenow," and "Frederick Grimké."

[24] C. V. Wedgwood, *Truth and Opinion* (New York: Macmillan Co., 1960), 14.

[25] Ward, Introduction to *Free Institutions* (Ward ed., 1968), 5.

[26] *See, e.g.,* as to Frederick, besides Professor Ward's Introduction, Arthur A. Ekirch, Jr., "Frederick Grimké: Advocate of Free Institutions," 11 *Journal of the History of Ideas* (1950): 75-92; and Maxwell Bloomfield, "Frederick Grimké and the Dynamics of Social Change," in *American Lawyers in a Changing Society* (Cambridge: Harvard Univ. Press, 1999), 235-70. As to the sisters, *see, e.g.* Elizabeth Ann Bartlett, ed., *Sarah Grimké, Letters on the Equality of the Sexes and Other Essays* (New Haven: Yale Univ. Press, 1988); Gerda Lerner, *The Grimké Sisters from South Carolina: Pioneers for Women's Rights and Abolition,* rev'd ed. (Chapel Hill: Univ. of N. Carolina Press, 2004); Pamela R. Durso, *The Power of Woman: The Life and Writings of Sarah Moore Grimke* (Macon, Georgia: Mercer Univ.

Press, 2003); Mark Perry, *Lift Up Thy Voice: The Grimké Family's Journey from Slaveholders to Civil Rights Leaders* (New York: Viking Press, 2001); and Larry Ceplair, ed., *The Public Years of Sarah and Angelina Grimké: Selected Writings, 1835-1839* (New York: Columbia Univ. Press, 1989). The "exception" is found in Gerda Lerner, "A Problem of Ascription," in *The Feminist Thought of Sarah Grimke* (New York: Oxford Univ. Press, 1998), 100-106, and is addressed below under the subheading "Frederick and Sarah in the 1850's."

[27] Lorri Glover, *All Our Relations: Blood Ties and Emotional Bonds Among the Early South Carolina Gentry* (Baltimore: Johns Hopkins University Press, 2000), 60.

[28] Ibid., 61. A standard, more generalized work is Stephen P. Bank and Michael D. Kahn, *The Sibling Bond*, 15th anniversary ed. (New York: Harper Collins, 1997).

[29] Lerner, *Grimke Sisters*, rev'd ed., 13-14. Lerner's account of Sarah's childhood draws extensively on Catherine Birney, *The Grimké Sisters: Sarah and Angelina Grimké, the First Women Advocates of Abolition and Women's Rights* (Boston: Lee & Sheppard, 1885). A friend of Sarah's in the latter's later life, Birney had access to some of the materials now in the Clements Library archive.

[30] See, e.g., David Potter, *Debating in the Colonial Chartered Colleges* (New York: Teachers College, Columbia University, 1944), 43-49.

[31] Edmund Sears, *The Gentle Puritan; a Life of Ezra Stiles,* (New Haven: Yale University Press, 1962), 365.

[32] Anson Phelps Stokes, *Memorials of Eminent Yale Men* (New Haven: Yale Univ. Press, 1914), 1:249.

[33] Thomas S. Grimké, *Oration on the Duties of Youth to Instructors and Themselves: the Importance of the Art of Speaking, and of Debating Societies. Delivered by Appointment before the Euphradian Society of the College of Charleston, August 13, 1832* (Charleston: E. A. Miller, 1832), 17.

[34] The examples are taken from Ezra Stiles, *The Literary Diary of Ezra Stiles*, Franklin Bowditch Dexter, ed., entries for Jun. 19 and Nov. 26, 1787 (New York: C. Scribner's Sons 1901), 3:267, 289; and Timothy Dwight, *President Dwight's Decisions of Questions Discussed by the Senior Class in Yale College, in 1813 and 1814*, ed. Theodore Dwight, Jr. (New York: Jonathan Levitt 1833), 4-5.

[35] Stiles, *Literary Diary,* entry for Aug. 23, 1771, 1:145-47.

[36] Ibid., entries for Mar. 5 and Apr. 9, 1782, 3:10, 15.

[37] Ibid., entry for Dec. 22, 1783, 3:102-03.

[38] Mary Wollstonecraft, *A Vindication of the Rights of Woman* (1792; repr., Quiet Vision Publishing, 2003), 156; Charles Maurice de Talleyrand-Périgord, *Rapport sur l'Instruction Publique* (Paris: Des Imprimeries de Baudouin et Du Pont, 1791).

[39] Stiles, *Literary Diary,* entries for Sep. 13-14, 20, 24 and Oct. 2, 1793, 3:502-03.

[40] Ibid., entry for Jul. 17, 1794, 3:527. Rehabilitated, Talleyrand would subsequently serve with notoriously shifting loyalties in a succession of revolutionary, imperial, and royal French governments, each of which found his diplomatic talents indispensable.

[41] Phi Beta Kappa Society, Alpha of Connecticut, *Minutes of Meetings, August, 1787-June, 1801,* entry for Jul. 1, 1794, Manuscripts and Archives Division, Yale University Library (hereinafter cited as "Yale M and A"). The July 19, 1792 Brothers in Unity debate is cited in David Potter, "The Literary Society," in *History of Speech Education in America,* ed. Karl L. Wallace (New York: Appleton-Century, 1954), 238-58, at 250.

[42] "Exercises at Commencement, Yale College, 1795," in *Yale College Commencement Programmes*, Catalog No. YY81, A2, 1812, Yale M and A.

[43] Benjamin Silliman, MS Diary, entry for Nov. 9-10, 1796, Yale M and A.

[44] See, e.g. *Scheme of the Exhibitions at the Public Commencement of Yale College, September 1, 1813* (oration on whether female education should include "the higher branches of science"), Yale M and A.

[45] Linonia Society, Secretary's Records, 1802-11, entries for Mar. 28, Jun. 20, Jun. 7, 1810, Yale M and A.

[46] Ibid., entries for Jul. 4, 25, 1810.

[47] Thomas S. Grimké, *On the Character of an Accomplished Orator, delivered in the South Carolina Society Room on the twenty eighth day of January, 1809* (Charleston: J. Hoff, 1809; repr. Early Am. Imprints, 2d ser., no. 17686); Thomas S. Grimké, *An Oration Delivered in St. Philip's Church, before the Inhabitants of Charleston, on the fourth of July, 1809* (Charleston: John Hoff, 1809; repr. *Early American Imprints*, 2d ser., no. 17687).

[48] *State ex rel. M'Cready v. Hunt*, 2 S.C.L. 291, 538 (1834).

[49] Maxwell Bloomfield, *American Lawyers in a Changing Society* (Cambridge: Harvard Univ. Press, 1976), 239-40.

[50] *History of Ross and Highland Counties, Ohio* (Cleveland: W. W. Williams, 1880), 79.

[51] Henry Holcomb Bennett, ed., *State Centennial History of the County of Ross (Ohio)* (1902; repr. Baltimore: Gateway Press, 1981), 1:170.

52 Mark Perry, *Lift Up Thy Voice: The Grimké Family's Journey from Slaveholders to Civil Rights Leaders* (New York: Viking Penguin, 2001), 48-49.

53 Ibid., 40-42.

54 *The Calumet, New Series of the Harbinger of Peace,* January-February 1835, 129-34.

55 Thomas Grimke, "Female Education," essay contained in newspaper clipping in the Weld-Grimké archive, unidentified as to the newspaper, with story on reverse side beginning: "Jan 4. Mr. John Quincy Adams presented to the House a petition for the abolition of slavery in the District of Columbia." He did that on January 4, 1836. John Quincy Adams, *Diary of John Quincy Adams,* ed. Allan Nevins (New York: Charles Scribner's Sons, 1951), 464.

56 Catherine H. Birney, *The Grimké Sisters, Sarah and Angelina, the First Women Advocates of Abolition and Women's Rights* (Boston: Lee & Shepard, 1885), 119.

57 Sarah to Theodore Weld, Jan. 21, 1838, in *Letters of Theodore Dwight Weld, Angelina Grimké Weld, and Sarah Grimké, 1822-1844,* ed. Gilbert H. Barnes and Dwight L. Dumond (New York: Appleton-Century Co., 1934), 2:518.

58 Birney, *Grimké Sisters,* 118. Birney's quotation does not give the date of Angelina's letter.

59 Thomas's opposition to a state senate resolution calling for a convention to lay the groundwork for a state Nullification act invalidating a federal tariff law, and his advocacy of that opposition in a published letter addressed to the Nullification measure's leading proponent, John C. Calhoun, "nearly cost him his life," Perry, *Lift Up Thy Voice,* 110.

60 *The Liberator,* Sep. 19, 1835.

61 Recounted in Perry, *Lift Up Thy Voice,* 114, 130-31, 145-46.

62 Sarah Grimké, "Condition of Women No. 3," notebook in the Weld-Grimké archive, 15-16.

63 Angelina to Weld, July 25, 1837.

64 Sarah Grimké, *Letters on the Equality of the Sexes and the Condition of Woman; Addressed to Mary S. Parker, President of the Boston Female Anti-Slavery Society* (1838); reprinted by Elizabeth Ann Bartlett in Sarah Grimke, *Letters on the Equality of the Sexes and Other Essays* (New Haven: Yale Univ. Press, 1988), and by Larry Ceplair in *The Public Years of Sarah and Angelina Grimké: Selected Writings 1835-1839* (New York: Columbia Univ. Press, 1989).

This work will hereinafter be cited to the Bartlett edition, in short form as shown in the endnote next following.

65 Sarah Grimké, *Letters* (Bartlett ed.) 31.

66 Sarah Grimké, *Letters* (Bartlett ed.), 57-58.

67 John C. Wright, ed., *Reports of Cases at Law and in Chancery Decided by the Supreme Court of Ohio During the Years 1831, 1832, 1833, 1834*, Preface (Columbus, Ohio: Isaac N. Whiting, 1835).

68 Frederick's Ohio Supreme Court opinions are reviewed in Maxwell Bloomfield, *American Lawyers in a Changing Society, 1776-1876* (Cambridge: Harvard Univ. Press, 1976), 249-54.

69 Perry, *Lift Up Thy Voice*, 196-97.

70 Lerner, *Grimké Sisters,* rev'd. ed., 223-24.

71 Sarah to Harriot Hunt, Mar. 18 [1853].

72 Lerner, *Grimké Sisters,* rev'd ed., 225.

73 Of Eagleswood, Birney recalled that "here gathered, at different times, many of the brightest, the broadest minds of the day . . . [her father] James G. Birney, Wm. H. Channing, Henry W. Bellows, O. B. Frothingham, Dr. Chapin, Wm. H. Furness. Wm. Cullen Bryant, the Collyers, Horace Greeley, Gerrit Smith, Moncure D. Conway, James Freeman Clarke, Joshua R. Giddings, Youmans, and a host of others . . . . Thoreau, also, spent many days at Eagleswood," Birney, *Grimké Sisters*, 272.

74 The letters are Frederick's to Sarah of Jun, 17, 1846 (referring to his visit to Belleville "a year ago last fall), and Apr. 30, 1859 (mentioning an 1851 visit).

75 Lerner, *Grimké Sisters,* rev'd ed., 245-46.

76 *Free Institutions* (Ward ed., 1968), 417-37.

77 Frederick to Sarah, Jun. 10, 1857, Jan. 30, 1858, Mar. 13, 1858, May 30, 1858, Apr. 30, 1859.

78 Meatless and consisting mostly of vegetables and wholegrains, the Graham diet would not have been tolerated in the Chillicothe establishments where Frederick boarded. His belief in eating moderately is expounded in letters to Sarah of Jun. 17, 1846 and Apr. 21, 1854.

79 Frederick to Sarah, letters dated Jun. 17, 1846 (recalls visit to Belleville "a year ago last fall"), Apr. 30 1859 (recalls visit in 1851, refers to others "during eight years"), Dec. 18, 1854 and Mar. 20, 1855 (visit to Eagleswood, fall, 1854); May 15, 1855 (about to leave for visit to Eagleswood); Nov. 13, 1855 (saw Sarah on visit to Boston, fall, 1855); Apr. 22, 1857 (visit to Eagleswood, summer or fall, 1856); May 30 and Nov. 23, 1858 (visit to Eagleswood, October, 1958); Dec. 14, 1859 (visit to Eagleswood, fall, 1859); Jan. 20, 1861 ("perhaps you may see me in the spring at Eagleswood").

80   Frederick to Sarah, Mar. 20, 1855.

81   Will of Frederick Grimke executed Sept. 1, 1862, Art. 8, Ross County Ohio Probate Court, Case No. 2769 (leaving his books to Angelina).

82   "A Problem of Ascription" in Lerner's *Feminist Thought,* 100-115, republished in Appendix II of her *Grimké Sisters,* rev'd ed., 297-309.

83   Frederick to Sarah, Nov. 23, 1858.

84   Lerner, *Feminist Thought,* 104; *Grimke Sisters,* rev'd ed., 300.

85   Frederick to Sarah, May 30, 1858.

86   Lerner, *Feminist Thought,* 104; *Grimké Sisters,* rev'd ed., 300.

87   Sarah to Hunt, Jun. 28, 1857.

88   Frederick to Sarah, Jul. 30, 1859, quoted in Lerner, *Feminist Thought,* 105; *Grimké Sisters,* 301. Frederick's writing often omitted question marks.

89   This mysteriously missing work on female suffrage might have been the one Sarah tried to read to a raucously inattentive audience at the Eighth National Women's Rights Convention held in New York City in May, 1856, the last occasion of her speaking in public. One of Sarah's notebooks in the Weld-Grimké archive, "Condition of Woman / No. 3," has a draft of her observations on suffrage.

90   Lerner, *Feminist Thought,* 105; G*rimké Sisters,* rev'd ed., 301.

91   Frederick to Sarah, Nov. 23, 1858. Perhaps Sarah did burn the letter, for no such document is found in the Weld-Grimké archive.

92   Frederick to Sarah, Apr. 21, 1854.

93   Frederick to Sarah, Feb. 20, 1857, Nov. 20, 1858.

94   Frederick to Sarah, Jun. 18, 1860.

95   Sarah to Harriot Hunt, Mar. 18 and Apr. 16, 1853; Frederick to Sarah, Nov. 13, 1855.

96   Lerner, *Feminist Thought,*105; Lerner, *Grimké Sisters,* rev'd ed., 301.

97   An example of a notebook passage Sarah addressed directly to readers reads: "I shall not lengthen this essay by entering into an argument . . . . One consideration however I must place before the reader, " Sarah Grimké, later "Education of Woman" notebook, 44-45.

98   Elizabeth Ann Bartlett, Note on the Editing Process, in Sarah Grimké, *Letters* (Bartlett ed.), ix.

99   Frederick to William Greene, Jun. 14 and Jul. 3, 1856, William Greene Letters, Cincinnati Historical Society.

100   Bloomfield, *American Lawyers,* 256.

101   On the claimed constitutional right of secession, *see, e.g.* William Rawle, *A View of the Constitution of the United States of America,* 1ˢᵗ ed. (Philadelphia: H. C. Carey and I. Lea, 1825), 295-301.

102   *Dred Scott v. Sandford,* 60 U.S. 393 (1857).

[103] *Free Institutions*, Book III, ch. vi: "The Institution of Slavery" (Ward ed., 1968), 417-37.

[104] Ward, introduction to *Free Institutions* (Ward ed., 1968), 12-13. For a contrasting view highlighting the treatise's "emphasis on the majority principle," see Arthur J. Ekirch, Jr., "Frederick Grimké: Advocate of Free Institutions," *Journal of the History of Ideas* 11 (January, 1950): 75-92, 79.

[105] *Free Institutions* (Ward ed., 1968), 118.

[106] Ibid, 200-01.

[107] Ibid, 117.

[108] Ibid, 122.

[109] Ibid, 28-29.

[110] Ibid, 133-34 (italics added).

[111] *Free Institutions* (1st ed. 1848), 71.

[112] In *The Proceedings of the Woman's Rights Convention held at Worcester, October 15th and 16th, 1851* (New York: Fowlers and Wells, 1852) Angelina is shown on page 5 as one of that convention's vice presidents, but a report on page 10 stating that a letter from her was read to the delegates suggests that she did not attend in person. In *The Proceedings of the Woman's Rights Convention, held at The Broadway Tabernacle, in the City of New York, Tuesday and Wednesday, Sept. 6th and 7th, 1853* (New York: Fowlers and Wells, 1853), Angelina is also shown as one of that convention's vice presidents, but the report makes no further reference to her participation. Professor Lerner mentioned Angelina's active participation in "the 1851 Rochester convention," Lerner, *Grimké Sisters*, rev'd ed., 239, but no published report has been found of any women's rights convention held that year in Rochester.

[113] *Proceedings of the Woman's Rights Convention, held at Syracuse, September 8, 9 & 10, 1852* (Syracuse: J. E. Masters, 1852), 92-93; *Proceedings of the Woman's Rights Convention, held at Worcester, October 15th and 16th, 1851* (New York: Fowlers and Wells, 1852), 111.

[114] Angelina to Paulina Davis, Sep. 7, 1852, published in *The Una*, Feb. 1., 1853; *Proceedings of the Woman's Rights Convention, held at Syracuse, September 8, 9 & 10, 1852* (Syracuse: J. E. Masters, 1852).

[115] Angelina Grimké, letter to the Syracuse Women's Rights Convention, *Proceedings of the Woman's Rights Convention, held at Syracuse, September 8, 9 & 10, 1852* (Syracuse: J. E. Masters, 1852), 81.

[116] Hunt, *Glances and Glimpses*, 291.

[117] Frederick to Sarah, Apr. 24, 1853.

[118] *Proceedings of the Woman's Rights Convention, held at Syracuse, September 8, 9 & 10, 1852* (Syracuse: J. E. Masters, 1852), 23, 28.

[119] Frederick to Sarah, Apr. 24, 1853, quoted with Angelina's capital "O" added to Frederick's "organization."

[120] *Rights of Women,* 21.

[121] *See, e.g.* William Lee Miller, *Arguing Against Slavery: John Quincy Adams and the Great Battle in the United States Congress* (New York: Vintage Books, 1995).

[122] Salem, Ohio *Anti-Slavery Bugle,* Mar. 30, 1850, quoted in *The Salem, Ohio 1850 Women's Rights Convention Proceedings,* ed. Robert W. Audretsch (Salem, Ohio: Salem Area Bicentennial Committee, 1976).

[123] R. A. S. Janney, letter to the women's rights convention held at Dayton, September 24, 1853, quoted in Elizabeth Cady Stanton, *History of Women's Suffrage* (New York: Fowler & Wells, 1881), 1:122.

[124] Ibid.

[125] Abstract of Annual Report of Ohio Women's Rights Society, *The Una,* Jul. 1, 1853, 86-87.

[126] *The Lily,* Apr. 1, May 1, 1854.

[127] *Free Institutions* (1st ed. 1848), 96.

[128] Karlyn Kohrs Campbell, *Man Cannot Speak for Her: A Critical Study of Early Feminist Rhetoric* (New York: Greenwood Press, 1989), 1:147-48.

[129] Gary L. Bunker, "Antebellum Cariacature and the Women's Sphere," *Journal of Women's History* 3 (Winter 1992):38.

[130] A popular history of one of the counties on Frederick's common pleas judicial circuit recounts an occasion when a "bevy of young ladies" playfully challenged his notorious aversion to female company by forming a human chain across a road leading into Chillicothe, intending to make him stop and converse with them on his way back from a ride in the country. "What an infernal set of fools!" he was heard to exclaim to himself as he turned his horse and rode off in the opposite direction. *History of Madison County, Ohio* (Chicago: W. H. Beers and Co., 1883), 397.

[131] Earlier "Education of Woman" notebook, 9.

[132] The page 351-52 treatise citation was mistakenly noted as ""251,2" in the page 19 notebook text.

[133] While initial entries in the later Education of Woman notebook text were written in ink, these *Free Institutions 2d* page 28-29 and 331 citations are in pencil, and thus appear to have been added subsequently.

[134] *Free Institutions 2d* page 598 contained Frederick's observation that:
"The number of idle persons is larger in Italy than in France. The younger sons are disinherited, feel little or no incentive to exertion, and live as they can, upon the pittance doled out to them by the eldest brother . . . .

[T]he abolition of primogeniture and entails in France, by placing men more on an equality, has driven them to greater self-exertion."

[135] Sarah Grimké, *Letters* (Bartlett ed.), 31.

[136] Earlier "Education of Woman" notebook, 14.

[137] Ibid., 13; *Free Institutions 2d*, 334-35.

[138] Later "Education of Woman" notebook, 37.

[139] Henry David Thoreau recalled meeting Cutler on a visit to Eagleswood in 1856. Henry David Thoreau, *Familiar Letters of Henry David Thoreau*, ed. F. B. Sanborn (Boston: Houghton-Mifflin Co. 1894), 335-38. Cutler's own letters – to Sarah Oct. 26, 1862 and to Angelina c. 1862-3, both in the Weld-Grimké archive – indicate later visits in the early 1860's.

[140] Added to the bottom of page 32, four pages before the beginning of her later Education of Woman notebook's answer to "why we desire an extended education," Cutler wrote:

I wish you would recast the form so as to say all that is to be said about education at once – that all of woman's wrongs by itself. There is now some confusion. By a rearrangement of matter the value of the essay would be enhanced. E. J. C.

[141] Nancy F. Cott, *The Bonds of Womanhood: "Women's Sphere" in New England, 1780-1835* (New Haven: Yale University Press, 1977), 5, 67. Note 7 on page 67 cites sources of the quoted expressions.

[142] Birney, *Grimké Sisters,* 276. Birney had access to some of Sarah's correspondence, but she does not mention when or to whom the quoted letter was written.

[143] Sarah Grimké, "Sisters of Charity," in Lerner, *Feminist* Thought, 132-48, and Bartlett, *Letters*, 154-64. The other "Condition of Woman" notebook, distinguished by "No. 3" appearing on the cover, was the source for a work Professor Bartlettt published as "Condition of Women," Bartlett, 126-33.

For Professor Lerner's identification of British feminist Anna Jameson's *Sisters of Charity and the Communion of Labour: Two Lectures on the Social Employments of Women* (rev. ed.; London: Longman, Brown, and Green, 1859) as the source of Sarah's work, *see* Gerda Lerner, "Sarah Grimké's 'Sisters of Charity,'" *Signs* 10 (Summer, 1985): 811-15.

[144] "Sisters of Charity," Lerner, *Feminist* Thought, 139, Bartlett, *Letters*, 156.

[145] Sarah's Diary, "First Book," Weld-Grimké archive, entries for May 15, 1821 (leaving for Philadelphia) and Sep. 15, 1822 (applying to join the Quakers); Sarah to Theodore Weld, Mar. 10, 1837, in Gilbert H. Barnes and Dwight L. Dumond, eds., *Letters of Theodore Dwight Weld, Angelina Grimké Weld and Sarah Grimké, 1822-1844* (New York: Appleton-Century Co. 1934), 1:373 (decision to leave the Quakers).

[146] Anna M. Speicher, *The Religious World of Anti-Slavery Women* (Syracuse, N. Y., Syracuse University Press, 2000), 5; Nancy F. Cott, *The Grounding of Modern Feminism* (New Haven: Yale University Press, 1987), 16; Blanche G. Hersh, *The Slavery of Sex: Feminist-Abolitionists in America* (Urbana: Univ. of Illinois Press, 1978), 136.

[147] Sarah Grimké, "Letter to Jeanne Deroin, Publisher of the [London] Women's Almanac," May 21, 1856, published in *The Lily* Aug. 15, 1856, reprinted in Lerner, *Feminist Thought*, 116-122.

[148] Sarah to Harriot Hunt, May 23, 1855. Sarah's dream was recounted in the note found attached to page 15 of her later *Education of Woman* notebook. Frederick's description of women's future as extending to the "engrossing occupations of life" is found in *Rights of Women*, at 33. "Mrs. Sockdollager" was quoted in a parody of a women's rights convention report, *Yankee Notions* (Aug, 1852), 1:237.

[149] Sarah Grimké, "earlier" Education of Woman" notebook, 13.

[150] In a March, 1852 letter published in the *Christian* Inquirer deploring the effect of early marriage in curtailing educational opportunities for women, Sarah wrote of "thousands . . . thus sacrificed, either by their parents or themselves, who, had they been educated in honorable independence [would thus have] been able to earn a livelihood by their own exertions." Letter from Sarah Grimke, Belleville, New Jersey, Feb. 10 [1852], *Christian Inquirer*, March 13, 1852.

[151] *Letter of Sarah Grimke to her Friend Gerrit Smith*, Eagleswood School, August 4, 1856, published in *The Lily*, Oct. 1, 1856. The letter is set forth in full in Appendix C.

[152] "The Women's Rights Convention," *New York Times,* May 15, 1858. The essay Sarah tried to read might have been on female suffrage, and based on views expressed in her "Condition of Woman - No. 3" notebook. A published version apparently ran in a journal, which Frederick in a Jul. 30, 1858 letter derided as "inferior" but did not identify.

[153] Martha Coffin Wright to Lucretia Mott, May 27, 1858, Sophia Smith Collection, Smith College Library.

[154] Frederick to Sarah, Jul. 30, 1859.

[155] Frederick to Sarah, Dec. 14, 1859.

[156] Frederick to Sarah, Apr. 21, 1854.

[157] Birney, *Grimké Sisters,* 276.

[158] Elizabeth Ann Bartlett, *Liberty, Equality, Sorority: the Origins and Interpretation of American Feminist Thought: Frances Wright, Sarah Grimke and Margaret Fuller* (Brooklyn, New York: Carlson Publishing, Inc. 1994), 81, 83.

[159] *See generally* Jennifer L. Weber, *Copperheads: The Rise and Fall of Lincoln's Opponents in the North* (Oxford: Oxford Univ. Press, 2006).

[160] *See, e.g.* Frank L. Klement, *The Limits of Dissent: Clement L. Vallandigham and the Civil War* ([Lexington, Ky.]: Univ. of Kentucky Press, 1970), 156-68.

[161] Sarah to Charles Stewart Weld, Mar. 16, 1863.

[162] Obituary of Frederick Grimke, *Chillicothe Scioto Gazette*, March 17, 1863.

[163] *History of Ross and Highland Counties, Ohio* (Cleveland: W. W. Williams, 1880), 79.

[164] Frederick to Sarah, Feb. 20, 1857.

[165] Frederick Grimke Probate Estate Records, First Account filed April 22, 1865, Ross County (Ohio) Probate Court Case No. 2769-A.

[166] Allen G. Thurman to Angelina Grimké, Aug. 13, 1863. Frederick's argument for the view that secession was a constitutional right is found in *Free Institutions,* Book IV, Chap. 2 (Ward ed,, 1968), 503-517.

[167] Thurman to Angelina, Jan. 20, 1866.

[168] Ibid.

[169] Robert D. Sawrey, *Dubious Victory: The Reconstruction Debate in Ohio* (Lexington, Ky.: Univ. of Kentucky Press, 1992), 4.

[170] Ibid., 114-16, 136-37, 142-43; Emilius O. Randall and Daniel J. Ryan, *History of Ohio: the Rise and Progress of an American State* (New York: Century Hist. Co., 1912-15), 4:304-307. U.S. senators were elected by state legislatures until the adoption of the Seventeenth Amendment in 1913.

[171] The slogan is said to have originated in a toast at the 1863 Ohio Democratic Convention, John Hare, "Allen G. Thurman: A Political Study" (PhD diss., Ohio State University, 1933), 127. For the Democrats' "new departure," see Randall and Ryan, *History of Ohio*, 4:309-10.

[172] Professor Ward's assertion that "the third edition was seen through the press by Grimke's sister, Sarah," is mistaken, Ward, "A Note on the Text," in *Free Institutions* (Ward ed., 1968), 40, n. 1. While in his letter of April 27, 1857 Frederick sent her a list of second edition "errata" to be corrected in her copy, there is no indication of Sarah's having had anything to do with the posthumous third edition's publication. In the same "Note on the Text" Ward states that he chose the second edition for his modern republication because it was "seen through the press by Grimke."

[173] George M. Waller, "Butler University," in *The Encyclopedia of Indianapolis*, ed. David J. Bodenhamer and Robert G. Barrows (Bloomington: Indiana University Press, 1994), 372-73.

[174] A similar bookplate is found in Yale University's presentation copy. A recent paperback facsimile edition was produced by Kessinger Publishing, LLC, in 2013, with the two volumes in separate covers.

[175] Frederick Grimke, *Naturaleza y Tendencia de las Instituciones Libres*, translated with an introduction by Florentino Gonzalez (Paris: Libreria de Rosa y Bouret, 1870).

[176] Ibid., introduction, iv. For translating the Spanish text of this and the immediately following quotation I am indebted to my law partner, Roman Arce.

[177] Ibid., introduction, i.

[178] William Whatley Pierson, Jr., "Foreign Influences on Venezuelan Political Thought, 1830-1930," *Hispanic American Historical Review* 15 (February 1934): 27-28.

[179] Katherine G. (Mrs. Frederick N.) Spinks (Thurman's granddaughter) to Watt P. Marchman, Director of Research, Rutherford B. Hayes Presidential Library, Oct. 11, 1948, letter on file at the Hayes Library.

[180] *Free Institutions* (Ward ed.), 122.

[181] See generally John Hare, "Allen G. Thurman: A Political Study" (Ph.D. diss., Ohio State University, 1933).

[182] "A Plain Duty," cartoon in *Puck*, Oct. 31, 1888, 160. For helping me find this image I am indebted to Clayton Lewis, Curator of the Clements Library's Graphics Division.

[183] *Free Institutions* (Ward ed., 1968), 138.

Index

www.ingramcontent.com/pod-product-compliance
Lightning Source LLC
Chambersburg PA
CBHW022249290526
45785CB00015B/480